T0247589

Praise for

TRUST THE BLUER SKIES

"Intimate and lyrical."

—**ANTHONY DE SA**, author of *Kicking the Sky*

"A luminous meditation on Portugal, family, childhood, and time: both evocative and wise."

—**MARK ABLEY**, author of *The Organist*

"*Trust the Bluer Skies* is a transcendentally stunning meditation on parenthood, community, and place. Crackling with wisdom and honesty, da costa reminds us that better is possible if we're only willing to imagine, if we're only willing to try. Deeply observed, evocative, brave, and full of promise. Memoir at its best."

—**ALI BRYAN**, author of *Coq*

"A portrait of the intimate bond between a father and his young son. paulo da costa guides his four-year-old and us through Vale da Cambra, Portugal, revealing his strong ties to family, his heritage and culture, and the landscape of his youth. He steers us to what he values in life now, eschewing the trappings of mainstream culture in favour of a less consumptive, peaceful existence. Engaging, inspiring, and always tender, this is a memoir to savour slowly."

—**ESMERALDA CABRAL**, author of *How to Clean a Fish: And Other Adventures in Portugal*

"There is a faith that propels *Trust the Bluer Skies*. Between the tradition-rich continuity of generations of a farming family sharing time and place, love, and birth and death, together all their lives, and the idealism of a radical gentleness that rejects religious conformity, exploitation of the land, men defined through aggression, and the killing of animals for food or sport, there lies a path to a nurturing and celebratory love that paulo da costa longs to see live between himself and his young son Koah. It is a revolutionary path, one man's work to change the meaning of father—for himself, his son, and us."

—**RICHARD HARRISON**, author of
On Not Losing My Father's Ashes in the Flood

"A father addresses his son using the second person, that intimate 'you' of epistolary correspondence that immediately plunges us into a direct conversation—an exchange that reads like a profound gesture of love, a desire for closeness. What we have in these narratives, these thoughtful utterances, is an insistence on bringing forward true communication between father and son, and also a keen aspiration to pass on cultural memory and knowledge from the paternal family line. Most importantly, these intimate articulations between father and son also call for change, turning away from traditions of masculinity and its recanting of emotion, which have plagued men the world over, and certainly Portugal, a country where manhood has been deeply ingrained in the social fabric, creating a homosocial ethic difficult to abate. In a lyrical, moving language, and with soulful skill and philosophical insight, *Trust the Bluer Skies: Mediations on Fatherhood* by paulo da costa invites us to let go of the chains that reduce our beingness and trust (and entrust in) our higher powers— those voices that inside us call to become a person, our individual self aching to be liberated from the weight of societal impositions."

—**IRENE MARQUES**, author of *Daria*
and *Uma Casa no Mundo*

trust the bluer skies

Meditations on Fatherhood

paulo da costa

 University of Regina Press

Printed and bound in Canada. The text of this book is printed on 100% post-
consumer recycled paper with earth-friendly vegetable-based inks.

Interior Art Work / Illustrations © by paulo da costa
Cover art: "Orange in a Tree" by psousa5 / Adobe Stock
Cover design: Duncan Campbell, University of Regina Press
Interior layout design: John van der Woude, J V D W Designs
Copyeditor: Crissy Calhoun
Proofreader: Kirsten Craven

Library and Archives Canada Cataloguing in Publication

Title: Trust the bluer skies : meditations on fatherhood / paulo da costa.
Names: da costa, paulo, author.
Identifiers: Canadiana (print) 20230581994 | Canadiana (ebook) 20230582060 |
    I S B N 9780889779952 (hardcover) | I S B N 9780889779921 (softcover) |
    I S B N 9780889779938 (P D F) | I S B N 9780889779945 (E P U B)
Subjects: L C S H : da costa, paulo—Travel—Portugal. | L C S H : da costa, paulo—
    Family. | L C S H : Portugal—Description and travel. | L C S H : Fatherhood. |
    L C S H : Father and child. | L C G F T : Creative nonfiction.
Classification: L C C P S 8557.A24 T78 2024 | D D C C814/.6—dc23

10 9 8 7 6 5 4 3 2 1

University of Regina Press, University of Regina
Regina, Saskatchewan, Canada, S 4S 0A2
T E L : (306) 585-4758 FAX : (306) 585-4699
U OF R PRESS   W E B : www.uofrpress.ca

We acknowledge the support of the Canada Council for the Arts for our
publishing program. We acknowledge the financial support of the Government of
Canada. / Nous reconnaissons l'appui financier du gouvernement du Canada. This
publication was made possible with support from Creative Saskatchewan's Book
Publishing Production Grant Program.

*This book is dedicated to those parenting,
their children, as well as their extended families
and communities that nurture them. We are
joined at the heart while navigating the challenging
waters of family and community life.
We are seeking to leave a better world for
those in our midst and those yet to arrive.*

Few people are capable of expressing with equanimity opinions which differ from the prejudices of their social environment.

—ALBERT EINSTEIN

We are, each of us, responsible for everyone and everything.

—FYODOR DOSTOEVSKY

contents

preface

Dear Koah,

During our family's six-month sojourn in Vale de Cambra—my childhood town in the northern, terraced, and grape-growing hills of Portugal—I began to scribble loose observations about your challenges while you were immersed in Portuguese customs.

I struggled, as I witnessed culture shock stretching out your psyche. I admired the strength of your four-year-old heart as the old skins of predictability peeled away and you endeavoured to blend into a new cultural landscape so very distinct from the quiet habitat of our Victoria home. You digested dissimilar world views and embraced or negotiated fresh ways to relate, without compromising your core being. For three of those months, you also had your first initiation to full-time kindergarten—another layer of change and challenge.

I marvelled at the lessons you integrated and the lessons you imparted. I watched the radiant smiles of adults and children touched by your kindness, courage, and compassion toward the vulnerable, be it a classmate or a neglected farm goat, a dandelion, a logged pine forest, or a broken adult heart.

After I gathered my notes scattered on pastry receipts, train tickets, and advertising flyers, a body of words emerged, and its meaningful contour became apparent. I wanted to leave a record of your experience in a faraway Portuguese town, a legacy for a time when you may wish to delve into your roots. Few of us remember events that transpired in our lives at the age of four. Those first years are formative for the personality and the spirit. Perhaps you will be interested in these glimpses, perhaps not. The choice will be yours. Although these notes and insights are personal, I hope they are also broader than us and reach beyond our tranquil Rio Caima eddies. These letters focus on our father-son relationship and also include your grandfather. At this time, it is the hope of many that the way boys and men understand themselves and relate will evolve for the better. Our present or future will not improve without reflection and consciousness, without a willingness to embrace alternatives, regardless of how they might be perceived from a place of stasis or age-old conventions. One cannot embark on a well-worn road and expect to arrive at a fresh destination.

These letters to you, intended to be read while navigating your young adult years, follow our family's journey through the cycle of cultural and religious celebrations in the northern, grape-growing hills of Portugal. You may one day stand before the mirror of these pages and accompany your younger self as you experienced your first sustained contact with your father's roots, finding your place among three living generations that embraced and loved you in a manner you had never experienced in Canada. In the vivid, memory-rich setting of my childhood valley, grandfather, father, and son explore our family history and digest the changes in the Portuguese and global masculine culture during the last nine decades.

Koah, I leave you these letters, these meditations on our multicultural family's sense of identity, culture, language, and the evolution of our extended family ties. It is my hope that those intense months in Vale de Cambra might have planted a seed of awareness that elevates you beyond assimilation and allows for the coexistence of multifaceted aspects of culture and languages, even within successive generations. Affective and linguistic ties can persist, wherever you might be in the world. They simply need to be attended to, cultivated and cherished for the added brightness and wisdom a collective memory adds to a child's sense of belonging.

These letters make no excuse for their piercing focus on our masculine experiences, as well as the father-son-grandfather relationships. I realize this will be a jolt to many. It is rare for a reader to encounter a book dedicated to the love and intimacies of fathers and sons. It is even rarer to be unapologetic about such focus. Your mother and sister are present, although not highlighted in these pages. Their conversations with you have their place outside the scope of this book.

And for you, intrepid reader, I welcome you to join our intimate father-son universe. This is my effort at setting out on a new road to deeper emotional connection in fatherhood; to transform our relationships with our sons. In connecting deeper to ourselves, in understanding our fears, we shall listen to our longings and therefore connect more profoundly with each other and the wider world.

All living beings may also appreciate the effort.

Be the world of one. Be one with the world.

paulo
Vale de Cambra, 2015

the oak grove

Fearless on your short four-year-old legs, your footsteps clap against asphalt and your knees nearly buckle racing down the forty-degree hill. I, too, ran down this steep lane, freed from the school day and sterile walls, and later I climbed even higher, further up the now-vanished woods to the high school on the crest of the hill. That was the first high school to be built higher than any church in the hills, signalling a change in the town and in the future of our lives.

I brought you from urban Canada to the village of my childhood to experience a taste of something that is dying. Of course, I have not told you this. It would sound dreadful and ominous. It has only been a few days since I started picking you up from kindergarten on foot, and you already look forward to the routine. First, we play in the schoolyard, chasing each other around the swings or racing down the slide. Sometimes you kick a ball around with your cousins Tomás and Simão who do not understand you when you answer them in English. When they tell the teacher, as they race through the tall iron gate, that they are winning, you reply, "We all win." This is a playground where everything is still about winning and losing. Happiness depends on who is first, who is last. You are brave to jump onto the high wire between cultures and languages, games and fears that are new to you. Rougher boys raised on a diet of TV cartoons filled with fistfuls of violence shouted and surrounded you when you arrived, turning you into a new exotic animal, attracting mobs of zoo-goers. Soon older boys will start pushing you to the ground and hitting you, and you will not tell me. Your cousins will.

After our run down the hill—which gives me vertigo staring down to its bottom, running down a lane where nobody wins but we have fun, a lane that in my childhood was a trail among the pines and oaks and turned into a spontaneous brook during the many winter days of rain—we turn right and follow the trail beside a section of the old irrigation channel that is four feet deep. The trail is narrow and the grass overgrown. There is a sense of adventure the instant our feet leave the asphalt and touch the moist grass that never dries out in winter. Your eyes widen when I tell you that in my childhood I fell into that channel a few times. Your grin seems to tell me you would not mind this adventure to turn wet today. You like risk and a change from the ordinary. As birds shuttle music to the fields, we bring the loud giggles and screeches, the stories and the leaps of those who turn the mundane into the miraculous. The women weeding in the field or the men pruning the vineyards stop and want to talk to us. The sight of children walking home from school is absent now; they disappear into vehicles that drive away. Those in the fields already know everything about us because news of our family of four staying in town has travelled faster than rumour. The rare farmers who remain here look forward to us enlivening their everyday now. The hills and the lanes without children are as quiet as birds without feathers in a butcher's window.

We leave the irrigation canal, and after a few turns on a crossroads of paved lanes, we stop at one of the many ditches carrying water to varied fields. We gather ribwort plantain leaves, wild daisies surviving in the shoulders of the fields, tangerines falling in hordes from the unharvested trees, and make them into racing boats. Our voices, quick breath, and occasional pokes coach their floating bodies down the stream emptying into the communal washing place that no longer seems to have anyone slapping clothes on its corrugated washing stone. Fewer chilblained hands in the neighbourhood as a result, I expect. Sometimes, the ribwort leaves entangle with the moss lining the stream in the way I entangle with the past, remembering the daily boat races of my childhood.

We stop at your grandparents, Micas and Agosto, for a late afternoon snack on the way to our apartment. You bring them the chirping aliveness of a being still in love with everything, wafting light upon the dark kitchen with walls three centuries thick. Your grandparents sit watching TV for most of the day; they wait for the news of the newly dead. In truth, they wait for the news of their own deaths, which will not be televised. Your joy brings a gust of wind into their slack sails. Without knowing it, you are already the highlight of their lives. Your grandparents do not want you to leave this town, this country, ever again. Our silence highlights what we all know: we shall return to Canada in a few months.

After you have kissed and hugged your grandparents, we walk to the yard and pick oranges from the tree to squeeze fresh juice. You always collect three times more oranges than necessary, twisting them in countless rotations until the stems let them go. We bring the fruit to our nostrils and relish the pungent citrus. Three bags of glowing suns perfume the air. Inside the house again, we bite into wood-fired buns and slices from wheels of cheese, followed by your soy yogurt, before we cross the lane to visit Tia Fernanda and Tio Zé Coelho on their farm, where we feed the goats our orange peels. For the sheep and the chickens, we smuggle collards from the field, a treat for the incarcerated.

We climb onto the tractor. Across the field, in the far distance, your great-uncle Zé hears your canto as a new bird in the fields and calls out, "Hi, Koah. Back from school?" He stops tying the vineyard shoots to the trellis with osier twigs and walks across the field in his heavy gumboots, glistening white stubble against a tanned creased face, to talk to us. Your great-aunt Fernanda, in a red floral apron, joins us from her work inside the house, offering roasted chestnuts still sweating into the blue winter sky. This is the place where your mere existence, Koah, is an event worth stopping for. This is a country where the heart reigns, not schedules, productivity, and efficiency. This is a valley of grey-haired farmers, where to be a child is still the most important occupation in the world and worthy of their attention. It's the same quality of attention they offer the corn seedling in the field, taking care not to step on it. Soon Fernanda and Zé have joined us playing with the chained dog, Bolinhas. The sun slides down the sky faster than we wish, and you help me harvest collards for the soup we will eat with doubled gusto later.

You may never remember these winter months, the hills and their eye-flinching green; you may remember instead that I took you away from your friends, your once-a-week kindergarten in Victoria, to experience something that was foreign to you and dying to me. I brought you to touch the land of your roots, to feel the blood that is moving across a people who have inhabited these hills and fields; I brought you to marvel at the pigeon-filled skies and the irrigation channels that have flowed for centuries. People here know who you are because they know the web of our family roots in this valley across time and have forgiven my absence for the past thirty years. The street sweeper is enlivened by your presence, released from her tedium by seeing us walk from school, and looks forward to crossing our paths even if she does not understand the excited English tumbling from your mouth. She absorbs the meaning from your bright hazel eyes, the dimples in your smile, and your gesticulating hands. Love pours out of everyone who stops to talk to you and acknowledges you are special for just being a child in love with the hills and the snails feasting on oranges.

This love is as old as the oak trees in the grove we pass after school, the only grove of trees remaining on this slope. I tell you of the time I was stuck on top of an oak, not knowing how to climb back down. I had climbed too high in my quest for a clear view above the hills that blocked the flight of my dreams. You stop and stare in awe at the ancient limbs as gnarled as the arthritic bones of the slow-moving woman leaning on an oak staff whom we just greeted. You stare at the tree. You stare at me. And you say nothing.

Days later, you share my tree story with your one-year-old sister, Amari, and with your mama, Heather, when they join us walking from school.

These are seeds of memory that you may never access from your own history. Your mother and I will carry this garland of memories to our graves. This is a history your parents and grandparents, aunts and cousins will carry in the family lore for you to hear later, if asked and if willing. This is a time when you do not yet fully comprehend the fortune of seeing grandparents alive and eager to receive your kisses, your embraces, in a country you may never live in again. During these five months, you will accomplish the work of angels.

On our route back from your school this afternoon, we pass by the oak grove where six people, wearing suits and hard hats, stand with maps in hand and sighting instruments pointing toward the main road that ends in a new subdivision, one hundred metres away.

"What are they doing, Papá?"

"I think they are discussing linking the road on the other side of the woods to the one we just left behind."

"These trees live here," you say loudly and in disbelief. The men look our way before resuming their measurements.

I nod in agreement.

Your pained expression makes my heart stop.

"The trees will be run over."

I cannot find the words to explain that people make terrible mistakes by not realizing the harm they cause. I cannot yet find the words to tell you they can do what they want to trees in this valley and they will do just that. It will be your first big loss in this country. A continuation of losses I have experienced in this landscape, cumulative biosphere losses. The black-and-white picture I saw in grandmother's photo album yesterday showed not a single building constructed from your grandparents' house to the school I attended, the same school you are attending. We now count more than forty houses on our path. Several of those are empty; emigrants decided never to return, while these paint-fading walls await their raison d'être, the fulfillment of their existence. A few houses wearing their bare red brick underwear are even unfinished. Others are vacant since their last elderly occupants, and the old skeletons of the houses have been left to collapse.

What can I say? I, too, run over my roots.

We stand listening to the ravens caw, bicker, and chase each other among the oaks. You lean your head on my hip and press your lips.

"The ravens will lose their home, too, won't they?"

I squeeze your hand.

In the distance, several terraces below, a little to the east, the small brown, white, and black dots of Ti Fernanda's goats bleat in their pasture. They have recognized your voice carried by the wind.

"Let's go and feed the goats," I suggest.

The road we follow makes a wide detour to reach the farm. We don't mind the extra time to follow the contour of the land, around the fields, along the irrigation channel. We spend more time together because of it. That is the reason we walked. There is much to learn every day in the lateral approaches to our destinations.

Many times I have wondered if letting you taste a dying world came with a price too dear to pay. There were times you clung to me with the clenched teeth of one drowning in fear, as you begged me to stay in class with you. On the first few mornings, I brought you in earlier, so we could become accustomed to the unheated rooms, the shouts of teachers herding the swarm of children interested in the exotic blond boy who spoke a different language. It was overwhelming for you and for us all in the family.

There had been a time when you experienced night terrors in Canada. We were concerned but did not feel guilty then. These days, when you scream in your sleep, my breath stops. You are free-falling without your Canadian friends, without a language to speak fluently, with cars driving too fast and not stopping at crosswalks; you are falling beside us, hand in hand, in order to land on the strongest web of roots you will likely ever encounter in your life. You are now for the first time living amid your extended Portuguese family. In Canada, you do not have any grandparents, uncles, aunts, or cousins; your mother's branch of the family has been pruned forever. There will be no more fruit.

When your mother and I die, your baby giggles and your tantrums will die with us. The formative details of the day you first touched sand and entered fearlessly into the ocean waves will die with us, and so will all the yet-to-tell stories of your beginnings. Some of us spend our adult lives searching for the echoes of that infancy (which rhymes with intimacy)—and these echoes set many of the directions in our lives. Most of us never fully discover those artifacts of memory. When we do unearth an echo, a smell, a blurred image, we vacillate. Often we wonder whether those memories are more art than facts. We attempt to reconstruct that edifice of childhood, the digging of our foundation. We wake up too late, after our parents have gone and left no stories to illuminate

8

the dusty one-dimensional picture albums. We wake up to our memories as late as we now realize we have awakened to our own present lives. Much has passed without meaning. Such key stories, such key memories open the door to our neuroses and our passions. They will release us. We need to learn where to find the key to those stories.

The truth is: none of these farmers and hills, these cornfields and old people were dying for you, my son. Not the grandparents, not the farming ways of life, the oaks, nor the empty fields touched only by the vanishing white-haired people stooped under the weight of memories. The *Silene stenophylla* flowers never died or disappeared unless we knew they had once existed. We do not mourn what we have never experienced. I do not know if the Portuguese language, which you fully understand and which you now begin to speak in a few longer sentences, will take root and bloom, or if it will become a distant, indiscernible echo in your memory. What I know is that many new windows into the world opened for you just as they were closing with the last breaths of a generation and of a time. I try not to have hopes. Yet I do. This time we are spending on the Cambra hills of my childhood is for you to savour and for the whims of circumstance and for the steering of your heart to decide what you will do with it.

If nothing more, I will take to my grave your smile as we stop every day to pick wild daisies from the edges of the cornfields and you carry them to the open hands of your grandparents and great-uncles and aunts who have not received the spontaneity of flowers since they dated five decades earlier. You do not distinguish gender in your affections, so we walked in the rain with a pink umbrella and a whistle. The umbrella was chosen by you at the biweekly outdoor market, never once dissuaded when the Roma woman in black attempted to convince you to take the blue. You never understood her distress. If nothing more, I'll take to my grave the memory of you asking me to touch the water running from the spring, cool and tickling your fingertips as any universe should tickle those still feeling. If nothing else, I will take to my grave the memory of treading the same ground with you where the bones of our ancestors have trodden for centuries, attending the same school grounds I attended, our faces recognized on the lanes by the elderly, holders of the living map of genes still populating this valley and these hills.

the stones
that anchor us

While your parents are alive,
it is better not to travel far away.
If you do travel, you should have a precise destination.

—CONFUCIUS

On your first visit to Portugal at nine months old, I carry you in my arms past the heavy wooden door, stooping a little so we do not hammer our heads, along with my tall ideas, on the low lintel. The door creaks, slightly scrapes the orange-yellow tile, announcing its daily labours, revealing a single wing that opens and closes time across generations.

It occurs to me as I first bring you through your grandparents' door that perhaps the Portuguese were not that much shorter three centuries ago. Most visitors must stoop through this doorway that delivers you to the kitchen, the heart of a Portuguese family home today, as in the 1700s when the house was likely built. Perhaps the builders intended dwellers and visitors to bow: a slowing down, a reverent tilt of respect and thankfulness for this shelter older than any living flesh or short-lived melancholic fado.

Our arrival sets the family voices talking simultaneously. Your cousins, uncles, and aunts surround us to kiss your cheeks, touch your glowing face, your amber hair. You cling to my neck. The kitchen grows rowdier. The boiling and frying sounds mingle with voices, bounce off the glazed tile walls and floor. The steam from the kale soup, from the salted cod fritters, the tomato rice, and the still-warm wheel of cornbread on the table meets the colder tile and mists the walls. Believe our elders when they tell us that a house can weep in happiness for those returning. They understand something about community that will keep you from the ache of loneliness. The voices continue to rise. No one hears anyone. Everyone giggles and shouts and laughs. Even you giggle and laugh, now more relaxed and beaming, happy to be passed from lap to lap. I am home, and you, too, are home for the first time.

We sit down to forget the pretend food offered on three plane rides, a twenty-four-hour journey through crosswinds, sleepless stars without sunrise or sunset, so as to arrive in Vale de Cambra. The conversation continues to reverberate, a catch-up, a fast-forwarding to bridge an eighteen-month absence.

"I do not see our Matos nose on Koah," your grandmother Micas says, raising her own straight nose.

Her piercing oak-coloured eyes, followed by every eye at the table, prompt you to turn toward me for reassurance.

"Lucky Koah," I say, winking at you.

The inevitable comparison of your face to our family facial tree arises.

"My, my…Koah's small nose, his honey-coloured hair, high cheekbones, and hazel eyes resemble no Matos," insists your grandmother Micas. But then she adds that maybe, just maybe, your spunk and glimmering eyes resemble mine.

"Koah's chubby cheeks take after great-grandfather Matos," says great-aunt Fernanda, perpetually tanned from her days in the cornfields.

Even your mother, Heather, does not escape comparisons, acquiring our genes by friction, I suppose, and is now stuck holding a resemblance to tetra-great-aunt Emilia, displaying her immortal red cheeks.

Four years later, it is your first December in Vale de Cambra. It is early afternoon, your grandmother Micas and aunt Marina, already awhirl in this kitchen, fry the *rabanada* baguette slices and the dumpling-shaped pumpkin *bilharacos* desserts that will crown the Christmas Eve table. Generations have assembled for a family meal among what were once walls of soot and bare wood beams but are now dressed up in an ornate '70s forest-green-and-beige tile pattern. The original earthen floor absorbed spills from the blackened iron cauldrons at the hearth, while today's spills pool on a steel-coloured propane range top.

While your baby sister, Amari, and Mama nap upstairs, you join your cousins getting in the way of the cooks' swirling legs as they loop from fridge to sink, to stove, to sink again, in pursuit of oil, butter, milk, eggs, or sugar.

You and cousins Tomás and Simão are asked to fetch oranges for freshly squeezed juice by Grandma Micas.

After we haul to the kitchen a bag that bulges with oranges, having added three lemons for good measure, I swing by a bowl of dried figs and walnuts harvested from Ti Fernanda's tree and swipe a handful into each pocket—emergency fuel for your yard play with Tomás and Simão.

"I'm bored," you proclaim, stretching your arms.

Again, we run outside with the cousins. Crossing the yard, we pass the persimmon tree, where unpicked fruit has fallen and mussed up the lawn with orange splatters that set me up for a skid. Four steps down to the next terraced field, the orange tree shines, displaying its own galaxy of one hundred suns. This is a blue-eyed December that lets us wear short sleeves rather than the season's usual three layers of clothing. The orchard bears fruit from trees your great-grandfather Manuel and, later, your grandfather Agosto planted. Even when I arrived from Angola at your age, it already glowed its seasonal colour palette from apple, plum, pear, orange, persimmon, and fig trees.

As you will, I have vivid childhood memories of this yard after life in a modern Luanda apartment. The ancient house, cumbersome and decrepit, rose higher than any other on the lane. Its L-shaped design hugged the west courtyard, where chickens scratched in the dirt below the Concord grape canopy and waited for the occasional raindrop of fruit. Their coop was tucked high off the ground in the womb of granite stairs that lead up to a second-floor entrance, which no longer exists. The chickens enjoyed their removable wooden runway that leaned on sticks and was wedged into the stone gaps. In this yard, I first encountered a beheaded chicken running and spurting blood in a last desperate breakaway from the dripping knife in Ti Emilia's hand. In her slow-motion chase, she cursed the bird's daring escape from the boiling vat, a curse for the loss of the precious blood that would have flavoured the traditional blood rice she cherished. Days later, foxes raided the roost; Ti Emilia had forgotten to shut the coop's wooden door for the night.

It isn't long before the kitchen door swings open; your grandmother Micas pokes her still remarkably grey-free head outside and calls, "Who can bring in a bucket of potatoes and an armful of collards?"

You race Simão to grab the blue plastic bucket from your grandmother's hand. Tomás sits down on the maroon portico steps, happy to enjoy a break and just watch the action. He retrieves a cookie from his jacket pocket, his plump cheeks filling up a little more. Bucket in hand, you race to the wine cellar where the harvested potatoes hibernate in vertical crate stacks. You and I fill the bucket, leave it by the kitchen door. Then I cross the lawn, step into the dew-laden garden. Before I finish tearing the collard leaves, you have moved your acrobatic leaps to the rim of the abandoned well that displays its clay vessels and amphorae. In March, tulips will paint a red ring around the foot of this well.

I toss you dried figs from my pocket. You gladly catch them. Acrobatics need fuel to run on. Your cousins prefer the chocolate I do not have.

When I was your age, the ground where I stand picking collard leaves was occupied by low-ceilinged corrals and the loom quarters, row buildings attached to the kitchen and stretching to the edge of the woods. The decomposing loom and spindle had already stopped weaving the passage of time by then; the only tapestries left were spun by spiders and glued themselves to my hair. In the pigs' corral, on a gap near its base, I emptied the stew of leftovers into the hollowed granite trough. It was in there, one morning, that I encountered a second death in the squealing of a pig. The cries pierced the stone walls and brought me racing down the outside stone stairs to meet four struggling men dragged by an Olympic-sized pig on a rope. The pig lost and was soon tied by the legs to a long wooden ladder, his pink throat slit. The pig bled into a clay vat painted with tiny almond flowers, while the scream decreased in pitch, in pulse, in power as the bloody stream, in time, drowned the voice; the body twitched for what seemed an eternity before silence reigned.

Through the door, I carry another table into the kitchen to accommodate the ten of us this Christmas Eve. Every stool and chair available in the house arrives in a convoy of hands to set up the banquet scene. Amari will occupy a wooden highchair that two generations of cousins have used. A long linen tablecloth woven in the now-defunct loom quarters alights on the two tables, making them one. Your grandfather Agosto stokes the fireplace with newspaper, pine cones, cardboard, and eucalyptus logs from the family woods, then sparks the matchstick.

Your aunt Marina and your grandmother Micas peel potatoes and wash collards, eschewing any help offered.

"Too many little bodies getting in our way."

They shoo us out with the wave of their dishcloths, lightly smacking our derrières and telling us to keep our hands off the food. "Leave room for the proper meal," they both say.

Until the dried salt cod finishes swimming to exhaustion in its boiling sea and the deep-fried bread and cinnamon have stopped sizzling in oil, we have time to play.

Now awake, your mother and baby sister join us in the yard. Amari's tentative steps on the uneven walkway approach the dozens of clay vases that line the walls. The front gate bell swings and clunks its metallic toll in the arcade, prompting you and your cousins to greet Ti Fernanda. She arrives from across the laneway with a tray of honeyed *formigos* for dessert. The family bread recipe, stewed in cinnamon, lemon peel, and honeyed red wine, is her specialty. Ti Fernanda disappears into the kitchen, emerging minutes later with a tray of prized *aletria* dessert and beaming her delight. Behind her, Grandma Micas also walks out for the first breath of fresh air in hours.

"Dinner's ready, children." Her high-pitched voice travels the yard and finds us taking turns on the portable swing set with Amari and your cousins.

At the kitchen table, the food exhales and sweats, appearing as exhausted as your grandmother Micas and aunt Marina. The walls have breathed the steam of boiling salted cod every December for three hundred years. The two women are not yet as still as the serving tureens. They wipe hands to their aprons, shuffle their feet, inspect the table, straightening a cloth serviette here, a dessert spoon there, ensuring that nothing has been forgotten.

The crunch, crunch of teeth cracks through deep crusts on cornbread chunks, with grooves resembling canyons on a moon. Your grandmother Micas stands by until forced to sit. She is too excited and exhausted to eat yet; instead she enjoys the pleased faces at the table, as they yum and wow with each forkful. "Just right." "Nice flaky cod." "Not too salty, not too bland." Tomás does not enjoy fish under any circumstance or miracle celebration, much less the dried salt cod variety. Instead, he clenches his underbite and turns his moon-round black eyes to the chimney, keeping watch for Santa's surreptitious tricks.

From the marble mantle in a corner of the kitchen, the moss nativity scene of hills with a flute-playing shepherd and the three kings watch our din at the table. The figures thank us for their clay ears. Throughout my childhood, a train looped around this green landscape, disappearing into a tunnel to emerge on the other side of the castle hill. In my child's mind, a train in ancient Bethlehem was not incongruent, and neither was a mossy forest landscape beside an arid desert with a biblical stable. Like many children, I followed along the tracks of belief.

Sprouting from the moss, a baby pine tree towers above the *presépio*; yellow, green, and red lights wink, casting bright colours on the faces of camel-riding kings, knee-flexing shepherds, white sheep, and herding dogs dotting the green landscape. Pulled cotton balls mimic the snow that valley children never touch in their winters. This year we could not find moss in the woods of my childhood, so we sought it on the embankments of a road farther away from town.

On this Christmas Eve, as in past centuries, the several courses of desserts arrive and disappear, until we swallow the last bite of sweet vermicelli or deep-fried cinnamon bread soaked in port wine. The adults slow their words at the table, unwilling to move after another Christmas Eve's excesses. For you, Amari, and your cousins, the best moment of tonight is yet to arrive.

"Hurry, hurry. The sooner the shoes are ready, the sooner Santa arrives," you say with little excited hops. Despite our dramatic protest, you three have already gathered a shoe from everyone to set by the upstairs fireplace, strategically placing the smaller shoes closer to Santa's landing. The nervous excitement running up and down stairs grows exponentially, riding on the sugar jolt from the king's fruit cake and honeyed *formigos*, the deep-fried pumpkin *bilharacos* and crème brûlée.

This year, I sneak away to dress up as the elusive Santa. Tomás, eight years wise, already suspects the old bearded reindeer-sleigh driver…until the lights go out to announce his arrival. I step into the kitchen from upstairs, hauling an empty red bag over my shoulder, stop to pretend surprise and awkwardness at encountering this family in the kitchen. Your jaws unglue, digesting the miracle. Chased by Tomás, I sprint up the fifteen stairs in four leaps, dash through the formal and rarely used dining room, exit by the tile porch staircase, leap over the railing before the last two steps—for an action, must-have effect, rooting the scene in Hollywood—just as Tomás sees me disappear into the night. I weave through the tree shadows to the *alpendre* on the east side of the house, repeatedly flicking the breakers on and off for a lightning farewell. When I return, I am wearing my civilian and mortal clothes, pretending I've been stuck inside the downstairs bathroom in the dark. I find Tomás and Simão with their mouths still agape from their encounter with living mythology, this time tangible. The shock-induced paralysis does not last once Uncle Filipe, limping on one shoe, wonders aloud whether in the commotion Santa remembered to leave presents in the shoes. "I surely can use my missing one," he sighs, sneaking a wink in my direction, one sock foot resting atop the other in a heron-like pose, displaying his own Santa's belly. The initial apprehension suggests disappointment, sets the small racing hearts stampeding up the stairs. Chaos ensues. Wrapping paper tears the air, fluttering to the rustic tile as red and green flakes.

The presents are opened; the toys, clothes, and games tried out. We return to the kitchen clutching favourites, ready for another round of desserts. Lying on the straw-filled manger and warmed perhaps by the breath of the clay donkey, but more likely warmed by the crackling flames from the fireplace, Baby Jesus lies sound asleep atop the mantle's *presépio*—its own miracle, considering our racket. Like Baby Jesus, other newborns have arrived for centuries within these walls. Your grandmother and two of her three siblings were the most recent births under this roof. It was here that she first encountered the soft winter light streaming through the naked grapevine canopy, bouncing off the room's blanched walls and assembling the first shapes in her retina.

Tonight, Christmas Eve, it is three hours after your regular bedtime, Koah. Your cousins have returned to their apartment for the night, and our family of four will sleep in my old room. Your eyes peruse the soft orange light casting kaleidoscope patterns on the ceiling. You ask me if there are ghosts in the room. Your sister falls asleep before her head touches the cold, damp sheets. I turn the radiator a notch higher. The house gargles. You giggle.

In pyjamas, bellies rounder from the previous night's indulgence, we nevertheless sit down at the orange Formica kitchen table. The mist rising from tearing tangerine peels with our hands freshens the air; the spiralling steam from the oats warms our chilled fingertips. We add chopped dried figs and walnuts from Ti Fernanda's tree. Having risen earlier than everyone, your grandfather Agosto already lies on the couch watching T V in the kitchen penumbra. We can see his warm breath clouding over in shock the moment it meets the cold. The dim grey winter light cannot cut through the metre-thick walls and Grandma's crocheted curtains on deep-seated windows. In summer, a pole is required to reach over the counters and turn the latch to bring in a breeze.

A skin of ash covers presents scattered by the fireplace, suggesting that the presents had aged overnight. Like you, I was four years old and just arrived from another country when I first stepped into this kitchen and marvelled at the open hearth, the fire under the blackened trivets boiling the turnip greens soup, the olive oil essence rising into the rafters of the naked red tile ceiling.

I smile, remembering my first Christmas in the Matos family house, placing my shoe by the soot-coated hearth, anxiously waiting for the appearance of Baby Jesus. I was disappointed when I found a small 45 rpm record of the Three Little Pigs by my slippers, certain He had mistakenly placed the large colourful 33 rpm Julie Andrews's *The Sound of Music* LP by great-aunt Fernanda's neighbouring high-heeled red shoe. I argued my best four-year-old geometry and the yet-to-arrive geocaching coordinates to sustain my argumentative thesis. Your great-aunt remained unconvinced, insisting she had requested that record in her letter to Baby Jesus. I asked her how He, still in diapers, could read. "Because He's God," she said, after some thought and twiddling her cat-eyed glasses. From that Christmas Eve onward, family members' shoes began a tradition of finding their fireplace location well, well away from mine.

After breakfast, you and I collect the torn Christmas wrapping paper from the cork room and cart it to the second cellar, where we store the salvageable paper for next year. My childhood bedroom furniture also lies here with the abandoned and unused Christmas trinkets from previous years. You admire the writing bureau and run your fingers on its walnut skin. I tell you that Grandfather

Agosto let me help with the design and construction of my bed, night table, and writing bureau, which I still cherish today. I remember his blue pen tracing straight lines on a checkered page, adorned by numbers and equations, as our vision emerged out of the cloud-like paper. Then we both sweated for the vision with the gnawing, gnawing of a saw. A dance of hands, a dance of father and son swinging arms toward each other, the blade's teeth chewing away, slicing through rings of time on the wood. A push and a let go. A let go and a push. Alternating strength and slack.

We move on to the yard again where I sit on the old discarded stone press, watching you pick more oranges from the tree. Here at your age, beneath the perfume of Concord grapes, I sat in the quiet, gazing at heart-shaped greenery, admiring the purple marbles that dangled from the sky. Your great-aunt Fernanda asked me why I gazed at nothing.

"I'm admiring the flowers hanging from the sky."

She looked up, squinted, and found nothing out of the ordinary.

"They are vine leaves," she finally said, smiling. "We don't eat them."

The morning has slipped away from us and already the alarms in our bellies ring, leading us to the kitchen for Christmas Day lunch. Your grandmother Micas still sleeps, recovering from yesterday's cooking and cleanup marathon. You set the table while I prepare leftovers: a mishmash of the boiled dry salt cod I debone, then tear up to join the sliced potatoes and chopped-up collards, all goldened in olive oil, garlic, and onion. It is tastier than the Christmas Eve boiled dish, and although everyone in the house prefers it to the traditional meal, my recurrent suggestion to instead eat this *roupa velha* (old clothing) for *consoada* remains a blasphemy. You lick your lips and ask for more crisp round slices of potato, not recognizing the reincarnation from yesterday's boiled variety you had cringed at. You are not so keen on the stringy cod, which you leave half-chewed to a ball at the edge of your plate.

The lunch flavours still linger on our palates as we step out of the kitchen door that creaks a little louder from a day of extra swinging as it welcomed visitors and flapped out of the way of children running through time. The sun lights up the persimmons and oranges on the trees, inviting us to the yard again to enjoy the festive mood. We sit on the portico tile steps, warmed by the sun. Christmas is likely the most peaceful twenty-four hours of the year. The air holds still. The lack of car and foot traffic in the lane confirms people are in their homes with their families as the day was conceived to be experienced. The birds sing, easily heard today, celebrating the gift of quiet.

earthworms
of the cosmos

Today is my day to listen. Amari pokes the freshly turned soil beside me, also listening. Her eyes remain wide in reverence for you, her four-year-old brother. Inside the house, Mamma Heather pushes the alabaster crocheted curtains apart, peeks from the window, and smiles at us in your grandparents' yard among the camelia, persimmon, and fig foliage.

Your index finger slides into the dark soil, turns it. A worm squirms, unsettled from her world, wondering if it could be her last moment.

"This is a casting," you say with confidence, lifting the finger to our gaze. My untrained eye detects only soil.

"Meee tooooo," Amari croons, moving her nose close to your open palm.

Nothing else exists in your universe aside from this ground and the worm in your hand. You run your fingertip along the dark underbelly of the worm, point to the castings in the wriggling body.

"Their poop makes the earth better," you say, tucking your shoulders to your ears and giggling. Then you caution us that only a worm's tail can separate safely.

"If you pull the rest of the body apart, it breaks. The worm will die." You raise your voice, nod with the slow motion of a solemn face.

Amari furrows her brows, concerned by the gory image. "Meee tooooo," Amari insists, thrilled to use half of her vocabulary.

After you brush your sunny hair from your eye, the earth trail on your face proves that you belong here amid the protruding roots of the fig tree. Tilting up your gaze from the soil and grass under your feet to look at your sister, you observe her tiny fingers digging, mimicking your gestures, seeking her own worm.

"It's wonderful to have such a little sister."

You sustain a silent space, and the blackbirds fill it with their opinions. They are crystalline. They are welcome.

"If I didn't have a sister, I would want one."

The sun cannot shine brighter than my smile after those words.

In time, you will be told how both of you are a sustained dream between your mother and me. A tenacity that at times appeared unattainable. In time, you will be told of your other brother and sister who never raked the earth with their fingers or giggled with the worms on their palms. Their birth placentas nourish the clematis vines and flowers climbing the deck railing in our Victoria home; they brighten and perfume our summers as their white eyes bloom every year to watch you play with your spades, shovels, and stones a mere breath away. Your brother and sister now help you fill the breath they could not draw in.

A butterfly alights on a flowering kale, draws our gaze. The wings flutter, leave a yellow trail that dissipates in another flutter of my eyelashes. Was it a mere impression of flight? Was it a dream?

You explain the butterfly's life cycle. The larva. The cocoon. You are wise and fluent in the metamorphosis of disappearances and reappearances.

Amari listens.

My heart twitches again with what-ifs.

Your siblings' ashes float where the Canadian rainforest and the Pacific salt waters meet. They rock in the same tides where twenty orcas greeted you on your first incursion into the wilderness, travelling on your mother's back. Those Sooke Basin waters are also where your grandmother Joyce's ashes had been swimming, so she at last could meet Robin and River in mutual longing.

You and Amari were born of our unwilting vision of family, after I cradled two newborn and unbreathing bodies in four years. Your mother and I held hands tighter and continued walking along a trail that threatened recurring loss. Giggles were not a guarantee at the end of that journey. Yet we never gave up hope of crossing paths with you, and later your sister.

After two heart-stopping pregnancies, each day of your gestation required deep breaths and stout bone. We insisted on having your birth at home. Many thought we were irresponsible, if not insane. Rather than shrinking before our difficult history, we were determined to change its course. You arrived early, at 7:07 a.m.

with serenity and jaguar eyes, while the sun rose that unusually hot September morning. Your wide gaze drank in the life denied your siblings laid songless beneath the hospital fluorescent lights. Under the stars and peeking moon, you breastfed in the last hot summer nights. You were a dream daring to stay.

As a child I, too, experienced losing a sibling, the unborn hope of company. I waited nearly a decade before your aunt Marina was born. Arriving too late to be a playmate, she became my baby, whom I helped bottle-feed, whose diapers I changed, and whose clothes I ironed.

You reach for your sister's hand, guiding her attention to the monarch butterfly. Gentle and loving, patient and caring. I smile. I cast a prayer to the stars: may the universe's powers allow you to have each other when I am riding a mote in the stardust of the galaxies.

Mamma walks down the tiled portico stair and watches you dig for worms before she breastfeeds Amari and takes her to nap. Amari stomps the ground in protest before being airlifted to her milky way of dreams.

You pick up a stomped-on daisy.

"What can I do now to help it?"

"Why don't you bury it?" I say, only half-present.

You stare at the limp flower twirling between your fingertips.

Moments later, you scratch the lawn with a twig. From scratch to groove, from groove to indentation, you deepen the scar on the ground.

"Have you decided to bury it in a hole?"

"No. I don't want it to die."

You stick the daisy upright and pad the soil around its foot. The flower droops. You walk into the kitchen and ask your grandmother Micas for a glass of water. With care, you make the cloudless day rain for the daisy.

The following morning, glass in hand, you kneel to the daisy and offer it more hope.

"It is not getting better, is it?" Lips clenched, you lift your gaze to meet mine.

I shake my head, rest my arm on your shoulder.

"Papá, I will cry when you die." You are about to sob.

"Oh, Koah." I shudder from the leap your mind has made. It is understandable. Every death is connected, a loss rippling.

"You'll die before me. You're older." Your eyes now swim, a rising tide of sadness.

"I hope that is true, Koah."

"Will you cry when your papá dies?" you ask.

"I will. I will be very sad."

"Why?"

"I will never be able to hold my papá's hand again."

I reach for your hand. You let mine rest over yours, feeling the weight, the warmth.

"Dead people lie like this." You shut your eyelids, place arms stiffly alongside your body, and lie still. Your face is dead serious. You could fool me. It is not a comfortable sight even in play.

"Papá, do dead people see each other?"

My head twitches in surprise. "I had never thought of that, Koah. I don't know the answer."

"When you die, I'll never see you again."

"When I die, I'll come to visit you."

"But I won't see you. You'll be dead. Invisible," you state, knitting the air with your arms.

"Is that what happens?"

"Yes, you go to the spirit world."

"Well, then I promise I will still visit your mind and have conversations with you whenever you invite me."

"But I won't hear you, Papá. You'll be invisible, remember?"

"I promise I'll get into your mind."

"How?" Your thin eyebrows rise, showing curiosity about my claim.

"Think of me, and I'll meet you. Since I will be a thin spirit, I'll get into your mind through your ear."

You smile, tickled by the unexpected solution.

"However, you must promise to stop resisting cleaning your ears." I tilt your head, pretend to inspect my route to your mind through the spiral of your ear. "Hmm," I rub my chin, exaggerating my concerns.

You appear worried.

"Right now I see a bog of yellow wax. I would get stuck and never reach your mind, Koah."

You roll on the grass from laughter, releasing the tension and worry in your body.

Instinctively, you swipe your sleeve across your nose, laugh even louder, rolling back and forth, clenching your belly. You cannot stop laughing.

Soon you become serious, stare me in the eye.

"You can visit anytime you want," you say, wriggling up along the grass beside me, snuggling to my chest and attempting to wrap your short arms around my neck.

My pinky finger props up the fallen daisy beside us. I see hope in your eyes. You are still at an age that believes in the superpowers of fathers.

The daisy falls to the side again.

This dead daisy that you have been attempting to resuscitate reminds me of the middle stanzas of the poem I wrote after you were born.

In the first hours, the smiles
and the flowers speak only

of the first light
to wash your eyes.

There will be another light
at your journey's end

that you will also not remember
offering no solace to your mourners.

This also happens to every flower,
even the ones spared in the fields

not prematurely severed
to mark ends and beginnings.

We gave you two gifts with one hand
although we will only speak of one

Death was present even in celebrating your tender life. The tango between life and death was born with and in you. Oblivion is no longer a choice for those of us who have held two deaths against our hearts well before their time.

The entrance's bell tolls, interrupting my reverie. You dash to open the metal gate. I sign the registered letter. After months of bureaucratic delay at the Vancouver consulate, after several follow-up trips to the registry in Cambra, Amari's Portuguese citizenship document has arrived. In the photo, her *chubbly* cheeks distort her face and her eyes appear nearly non-existent. We chuckle. You ask to see your card, ensuring you do not share her outsized suckling cheeks of a trombone player.

You hold both ID cards side by side.

"What does mine say?" you ask.

"Koah Skye Soares Matos Steel da Costa."

"That is a stretchy name."

You sing the train length of your name, making it into a song with enough crescendos and diminuendos to turn it into a one-line opera.

"It names both ancient and recent branches of our family tree, Koah. From vovó and vovô's side of the family. The Steel is from your Scottish grandfather, Robert."

You are silent now, proud as one who has arrived at a long road already in motion, guided by the steadfast signposts to carry onward.

"That way you cannot be lost in this Cambra valley or in the vast ocean currents of the world wherever they might take you. Everyone here will know who you are related to."

A blackbird darts from the fig tree and lands in the kale patch. It pecks at the soil and flies up to a branch, hauling a wriggling worm in its beak. This worm will not survive the breakup from an incisive beak. The robins sing in jubilation.

In the Canada that welcomed me in the '80s, my first three identification documents did not provide sufficient space for my complete name. The bureaucracies initialized my middle name or one of the family names, then chopped off half of my last name. Medical and administrative appointments still turn into a detective nightmare to locate me in databases. Which last name am I listed under? In Canada, the available characters, the available space for memory, the available space for past connections leaves me dangling. I am Mr. Co. Apropos for the severing of my homeland roots.

Matters have improved in recent decades. Being Canadian born, Koah, your SIN shows your six names; however, you are only allowed three last names. For us subsequent settlers after conquest, Canadian family roots do not sink that deep into the earth yet. So, we are forced to turn *Soares* into another middle name so as not to sever your grandmother's lineage. Logging remains a primary industry in our nation of forests, even when it refers to family trees. Memory extraction is a strategic industry of acculturation to repave the landscape of belonging and memory.

Perhaps one day your children will be permitted more space to bring their extended family roots along, and the songs of their names will unreservedly spill from their tongues. It will help them remember they exist beyond confined government identities.

You have returned to digging the soft ground for worms. The anticipation of finding a new story propels you onward. An ant's strength draws our gaze into the grass. In silence we watch the ant haul an oak leaf blown in from Ti Fernanda's yard across the lane. The ant will carry the leaf toward the hunger of the colony.

It could be the blackbirds' aria, or the damp soil between your toes; it could be the rippling green kale leaves awash in your pupils, or the scent of grass under your fingernails digging for worms that root in your mind, that make you an archeologist immersed in infinity, unearthing the fragments that piece together our common Portuguese past.

Already you are this proud future standing elsewhere from my roots and cherishing the seeds and values of a past. You are not taking memories for granted. Absence is often more present for the vacuum it leaves: the absence of grandparents, great-uncles, aunts, and cousins, whose presence your Victoria friends enjoy. The warmth and memory of family are already a longing in you. You prompt us to collective hugs, weekend adventures. Wisely, you understand the need to assemble an extended clan to repair the tear of distance you inherited. A reimagined family will bridge the many distances I have created for your future. There is the distance of time to your older parents, and the geographic distance between continents to your extended family and to your Portuguese roots.

The blackbirds shuttle to and from the fig and plum trees. At our feet, another worm and the fallen daisy meet.

"Do worms eat flowers?" I ask.

You laugh.

I lift my eyebrows, widen my eyes.

"They eat you, silly."

Your wild laugh rises into the sky as birds toss their songs in the trees. I join in, and together we laugh our one-line opera of existence that has no words, yet resembles a long family name.

grandfather
swallowed the clouds

You run into the tiled kitchen, trailing the scent of daffodils, and invite your grandfather Agosto outside. "Come, come. Let's play hide-and-seek." Your small hand finds his calloused fingers under the wool blanket, pulling his arm away from the vinyl couch, where he lies for most of the day. He says he can't; he fears the cold drafts, fears the sun's intensity. In his eighties, he is afraid of most things. Wide-eyed, you assure him the outside cannot possibly hurt him. "The sun only tickles your skin a little. It's nice." Your grandfather avoids your expectant eyes and seals his again. Disappointed, you accept his refusal; yet today is not a day you will sit on the couch with him as he changes the channel to cartoons, though that sitting in each other's company, without talking, would still be a type of blessing.

Your grandfather Agosto fears death, and unlike your grandmother Micas, who prays the rosary nightly and attends mass once a week, he has not found a spiritual cane to aid his mind in those last steps toward stillness. In view of the tightly shut lids and the frown on his face, he is again travelling through his landscape of worries. Declining your invitation to play will become another heaviness in his endless inventory of panics, failures, and inadequacies of old age; it will make him slip further into his well of darkness. He remembers himself differently, as others in this valley do. He remembers himself without weight on his bones or mind, free to run with your aunt Marina and me on the beach, to bodysurf the ocean breakers. He is unable to shake the unexplainable weight in his mind by riding the fresh spring wind that you are, by basking in the glowing and bright smile that never fades.

Your four-year-old limbs seek movement, speed, and the quivering of laughter. In such moments, I am reminded of the consequences of my belated parenthood. I show you a younger *avô* Agosto and *avó* Micas in a portrait before my existence, and you do not recognize them. Your mischievous grin tells me you file this moment on the father's joker list, as when I point to invisible dinosaur bones on the bare field-terraces as we walk home from school. "Can you see the tyrannosaur jawbone?" I say, pointing high on the embankment. "Higher up, over there." Naturally, no one can see it, except your cousin Simão, who does not like to lose face even while seeking an invisible bone.

One day I will tell you that Grandpa and Grandma were not always the octogenarians you will remember them as. You arrived late, yet not too late. On the other hand, I arrived too late for a grandmother who left early with stomach cancer. Life is made of these absences and unmeetings. I encountered her through stories, the way you now meet your once-younger grandparents through my accounts while looking at their corrugated frowns that slow their thoughts. Soon you will be able to imagine other lives for them, even though you are not a character in those earlier tales.

Today, it is your grandmother Micas who, hearing your plea to play, joins us at hide-and-seek. She leaves behind her reinforced kitchen chair. Trembling, she walks stiffly away from her advanced Parkinson's disease and overweight body, away from her diabetes and litany of other ailments. Mostly, she stands in a corner or behind the imported cedar tree, highly visible. She requires help getting back to her feet when she kneels behind a rose bush. You understand and help in the same way you make those allowances for one-year-old Amari, unstoppable in her tiny steps and continuous stumbles.

Only seven years ago, your grandfather Agosto spent his days pushing your cousin Tomás in his plastic four-wheel jeep—endless laps around the courtyard, occasionally exiting the gates for a next-door visit to Ti Fernanda and Ti Zé's farm. When Tomás learned to walk, the two would kick a football back and forth. For three years, your aunt Marina arrived home from her bank job eager to play with her son, only to tuck your already asleep cousin in bed. Then his brother, Simão, was born, and Tomás entered kindergarten. The cycle had again begun.

Tomás was a gift to your grandfather's empty days and a return to a semblance of parenthood he had missed, as most working fathers do. This time together wove a unique and enduring bond between Tomás and your grandfather Agosto. It is still a common bond in this valley where grandparents, if retired, take over the task of parenting from their overworked adult children. Your aunt Marina was absent for excessively long hours, working in another city, an hour away on a lucky traffic day. This is the new world of progress that expects loyalty to corporations first and where, despite legislation for parental leave, workers understand they cannot enjoy full rights or they will lose their jobs. Every week, in exchange for sixty hours of her life, your aunt can choose the brand and colour of a fancy stroller, a room full of toys, a gigantic flat-screen TV.

In his seventies then, timing and circumstance gifted your grandfather Agosto with a surrogate fatherhood at an age when he could barely summon enough energy to match the exuberance of a young child. "Now, it is a different story," he confided in the tone of an excuse and a sorrow, looking at you chasing a fly around the kitchen table. "Each new decade arrives weighing as much on my bones as a whole new century."

In this Cambra valley, the presence of uncles, aunts, and grandparents in a child's universe is taken for granted. It causes me to ponder the empty clan legacy you experience in Canada.

You will live most of your life without grandparents in your day-to-day. You will live most of your life without a father and mother. Your children, if you choose to have them, will likely live without at least one set of grandparents, as you did. If I am fortunate enough to meet those grandchildren, they will still lose me too young to remember me as a grandfather.

The transmission of family lore and values to grandchildren is achieved in short time windows, and I'll miss important seasons of life as an absent elder. The side-by-side modelling that allows the young to learn by osmosis, and to move through the planet in the family bosom, will not be feasible for us, son. I suggest you adopt substitute parents and grandparents for the emotional balancing the elderly occupy in the psyche of an extended family. It is an underestimated elixir of wisdom when such a relationship is healthy, loving, and inspiring.

It is another afternoon after kindergarten, and for a moment, you look puzzled by your grandfather's sad face as he declines another invitation to play. "Vovô won't play with me." You drag your feet toward me, shoulders wilted. Unbeknownst to you, it is the clouds he has swallowed that have darkened his days. These clouds now block his once-visible radiance. They obstruct the light breeze that could air his mind and sweep away the heaviest trapped thoughts. Clouds gone unswept for a decade have transformed my jovial and playful father into an absent grandfather whose main profession is to worry, to complain. Your grandfather worries that sneezes are an early cancer warning, that a light bulb left on will bankrupt him, that a counting mistake in the daily home delivery of bread buns signals Armageddon. He swallows many colourful pills and asks his doctor for more. Unknowingly, like many, he seeks the blue-green pill of happiness, that chimera of science that promises to deliver, without effort, the memory of where he dropped the light that once illuminated his path. Your grandfather Agosto struggles with an ailment most cannot see, although you can feel it.

You have met only one of your grandfather's many lives and seasons. You will meet his other selves in the stories yet to surface as you grow up. You already seek these stories at bedtime, and you marvel at the black-and-white photos of him in military airplane cockpits and heavy flight gear that makes him resemble an astronaut.

"Did Vovô fly to the moon?"

I smile. "Just to the clouds."

In admiration, you nod and raise your gaze, attempting to measure the height. The low ceiling cuts short the flight of your gaze.

When your grandfather Agosto closes his eyes to you on the kitchen couch, the facial tension and teeth clenching draw a picture of pain I do not recognize from his good-natured days brightened by his sparkly pupils. You can teach anyone to laugh with your trickster mind, yet even you cannot move someone invested in their unhappiness. You look at me and shrug. It is not you, I know. Your grandfather has unlearned how to laugh.

I toss the ball. It bounces off your shoulder. "You're it," I say, running out the kitchen door into the yard. You follow in nimble leaps to catch up to your favourite freeze-tag handball game. You laugh for a continuous hour as we play in the yard, and you roll on the grass after every tag, dramatizing the fall.

Nevertheless, day after day, you do not give up on your grandfather and continue to pick a wildflower from the fields on your way back from school. Then you run to him, stretched out on the kitchen couch. "Smell, smell it. It's delicious." He stirs from his slumber and lets you bring the flower to his nostrils. He agrees and attempts a smile. You delight in his agreement. I already admire your resilience in this relationship and imagine that this rare trait of not giving up on people will bring you much love and esteem.

The tulips and daffodils have begun to trust the bluer skies and open their petals when your grandfather comes out of the kitchen. He joins us as we sit on the warm tiled portico, enjoying an after-school picnic with your cousins and Amari. In his hand, he carries a solid lead-cast de Havilland Chipmunk model as if it were flying in midair. This is the plane he first piloted in Portuguese Air Force missions in the '60s. He painted the model true to its red nose on the grey body, down to the white coat of arms with its seven castles on the tail. He keeps the model in the cork-insulated TV room next to his portrait in full uniform—a hat and suit decorated with medals—which always manages to stop you in your tracks despite the rush to your hide-and-seek games. Your grandfather remembered your earlier request to see "the real plane Vovô used to fly." I know you had been hoping for the full-sized aircraft, so you could jump to the commands and mimic the growl of Ti Zé's tractor next door, shifting gears, your body in full stretch to reach the pedals. You smile. "It's heavy." Your grandfather is pleased by your fascination with his Air Force flying times, the high point of his life, and that you ask for stories. He stays a little longer, until a breeze arrives and he retreats, afraid the wind might steal him forever away from his grandchildren.

Today, the wind did not rise. Instead, your grandfather Agosto rose from the couch to join us for a stroll in his much-loved woods. "Vovô is coming out. Vovô is coming out." You climb up and down the tiled portico stairs outside the kitchen entrance, running from me to him, from him to me, until he puts his coat and brown hat on. Then you stand very close to him, holding his hand as we walk to the car. After a ten-minute drive to the adjacent county, we stop by the farmhouse where he was born.

We walk away from the house to the woodlot he owns and which one day may be yours.

Your grandfather paces his words to his slow steps. He tells his once-upon-a-time stories of walking these hills to school, barefoot, rain or shine, light or dark, as days shrank and lengthened.

I let you absorb the significance of such an unimaginable world. Quiet, you stare at your light-flashing runners stepping over jagged stones and prickly furze while listening to the stories that make the past visible.

"Barefoot to school, rain or shine, six kilometres each way." He emphasises the feat.

"All alone?"

Your grandfather Agosto nods solemnly. The wrinkles on his forehead deepen.

"Why didn't your mommy go with you?"

The frown grows more visible in your face.

"Every kid walked to school and back by themselves in those days," I interject.

You look at me with the face of "That is not a good reason or answer."

"Back then, there were no speedy cars or constantly busy roads to make walking dangerous. Parents didn't worry about little ones crossing the roads," I say, highlighting the points you can understand.

For a grandfather who seldom talks, this unending spring of stories flowering from his mouth surprises you. Another grandfather is born in your eyes. This is the man I recognize from my childhood, who would delight a table of guests and family with tales well into the afternoon, until new plates arrived for another meal of leftovers, as the day refused to end.

"I read my school books by olive oil lamps and candlelight. Electricity arrived at our house when I was eleven," he continues.

Two stone walls line the paved lane we climb. Smoke drifts from neighbouring chimneys. A few houses still leave their fireplaces burning through the spring day. We reach the lip of the rise where the paved lane ends, and a clay trail begins to carry us to the parcelled woods. Here the lots are divided by low stone hedges. Your grandfather's woodlot lies on a steep north-south grade ending at a stream. The trees are mostly eucalyptus. The once-lush hill is dry even now, at the start of spring. The moss carpets I remember collecting at Christmas for the nativity scene under the decorated pine tree are no longer.

"I was gifted these woods when I was Amari's age." He smiles, tickled by revisiting the thought, the luck that dropped in his lap. "For his birthday, my brother, António, was given the choice of a guitar or these woods." His older and only brother did not hesitate. He was twelve.

I observe you with curiosity. I, too, heard that story from waist-high times, and I remember the embedded warning. Guitars are ephemeral. Eight decades later, these woods still stand, turning trees into cash and providing a piece of the earth to his name. Our family in Canada does not own woods.

"Where is the guitar?" you ask him.

"Who knows where the guitar is now?" your grandfather says, surprised anyone would want to know its whereabouts. I know you do. You already strum your cousin Tomás's toy guitar, the one missing a string. Decades earlier, I asked the same question.

"If your godfather had placed a tin of chocolates next to a blue land registry document stating you could own a chunk of woods, what would a four-year-old choose?" I say, winking.

Grandfather Agosto stares at the sky that is no longer alone with the birds. This once-upon-a-time dirt trail, wide enough for ox-pulled carts to haul the trees away, has been paved over. Gigantic utility towers overwhelm the tree canopy, and high-voltage power lines hover above the property, stunting the reach of the eucalyptus. Unlike the disappeared song of crickets or frogs, the humming power lines offer no pause, no reprieve of silence. There is no season to their song. They never, never sleep.

While digging his foot in the thick deadfall, Grandfather Agosto entangles his leg and loses his balance. You look with apprehension. I catch him in time. Attempting to free his foot again amid the piles of dry eucalyptus branches and leaves, he clears his throat. He enjoys inspecting the ground for the half-buried boulders that mark property boundaries, a task from older times when increasing a holding area meant a simple pick-and-hoe job under the cover of night.

Grandfather Agosto reweaves the thread of his memories on the farm.

"After school, I carried my books in my satchel and took the oxen to graze in the woods. They appreciated gorse and ferns and grasses. They helped keep the hills clean. I do not have a memory of a forest fire in our lands then."

Concerned by the thousands of hectares that burn every summer, Grandpa is alluding to the fires that plague Portuguese woods. Most are set fires. The pulp trucks arrive soon after so as to bid on the charred eucalyptus at bargain prices. The deep charring on a few large stumps reveals the devastating fire that swept through his woods a handful of years ago.

Within sight of the woods, the terraced farm that raised him perches on the hillside. Over hundreds of years, a staircase of fields was carved out from the forest. Now, a twin highway axes off its feet. I tell you of a disappeared field, its canopy of grapes over the collards, in a time when the road was slender and of cobblestone, skirting the swamp, where I harvested *uvas americanas* to the croaking of frogs, where watercress grew for our Saturday salad. The swamp and frogs, grapes and geckos laid to rest under a blank of asphalt now require you to imagine what you have never seen. The chirping of birds at the farm has been replaced by the zoom of cars. A song that is not a song, and it never ends. The land will sleep for a long, long time. The asphalt will be seen for the crude entombing of the earth that it is, and one day it shall be digested by the rising up of the soil, reawakening.

The last bite of the after-school snack of crisp bread and sheep's cheese still churning in your mouth, we step outside the dark kitchen to play, while your grandfather Agosto snoozes on the couch.

Your laughter is the loudest bird call in the yard, as we play freeze-tag handball and occasionally roll on the grass to catch our breath, staring at the blue sky. The high-pitch pleasure brings the curious crows to the camellia treetop. The birds join in and caw.

The kitchen door opens. The low afternoon spring sun dares to enter the doorway. Your grandfather Agosto draws a chair to the pool of light and rolls up his pant legs, letting the marble-coloured thin limbs be kissed by the warmth. He rotates the chair a little so he may follow our game and eavesdrop on the laughter pouring into the kitchen. I catch your attention and nod toward the door. Only his glowing white legs show in the dark of the kitchen. You giggle. I wink. Your grandfather has arrived, cautious as a curious fox in the forest, willing to learn laughter again. It is the only trick that will fool death.

I point at the sky. "Here comes a spitfire dragon." Distracted by my call, you look up. I toss the ball. It bounces off your forehead. *Boomp*. You are tagged. Tricked again, you smile, then growl, tackling me to the ground where we roll on the grass and spill our laughter like flower seeds ready to take root in your grandfather's garden.

bones

Three men clutch black fedoras against their chests and talk in hushed voices. This murmur of people congregated around the coffee shop window draws your attention.

"What are they reading, Papá?" You point to the two notices bordered in thick black, attracting their interest. Writing is a code, a magical language between adults, offering access to mysterious information and therefore a power as yet outside your reach.

People heading to work have converged at the cafés for their on-the-run coffee. They will allot more time to surveying the café windows filled with notices, among them sombre news, framed in solid black borders, listing the freshly dead. Photographs stare back at the eyes searching for signs of recognition. The elderly know one another from growing up at a time when this city was a small Portuguese town with the spirit of a village. Everybody knew everybody. They might not have exchanged a recent word with the deceased, or perhaps ever, yet they will identify which extended family now is left behind. The notices list the names of those related and unexpectedly in mourning. If the poster face before the onlookers' eyes is closer to their affections, they will be jolted by death infiltrating their networks of café comradeship. They will recall their last conversation or greeting. Two days later, the church bell will toll during the funeral procession to the graveyard.

"What are the three men reading, Papá?" you repeat and pull my arm as I, too, read the notice and become lost in thoughts of death. I do not know these two unrelated people, who have passed away on the same night.

"They are reading the names of people who have died."

"How did they die?"

I glance over the stooped shoulders in front of me and see two faces that look far younger than the notice states: "sixties and seventies."

"They were old," I assure you, although in my mind they are not old. By my count, I am not that far off the tally.

I have yet to see a person under forty stop to identify the dead gazes posted on windows. It is a daily ritual to those smelling death in the morning air. Those older and retired will stay behind a little longer, talking to each other about their memories of the deceased. "A good man." "A troubled family." Sometimes they are left to guess the cause of death; other times they already know the name of the eroding cancer. Our valley counts among its achievements the highest incidence of cancer in Portugal. People accept the honour with a shrug, the same way they accept other collateral damage from their employment as the price of eating. The death plague settled over this valley after the metallurgical and pesticide canister industry mushroomed amid the farming community in these once-greener hills.

The factories wait for darkness to release their toxins. The sweetened midnight air too often reeks of insecticide and drifts away above the valley on a westerly. On unlucky nights, the poison remains trapped between the bosoms of the hills and comes to rest over the Vigues, Moscoso, and Caima Rivers, on the fields and crops, on people's backyard fruit trees and vegetable plots, on the water reservoir. The night flushes of the metallurgical industries' pipes into streams meet the nightmares of the young. The rivers will in time find every water tap and glass, touch the lips of old and young. The invisible weight of heavy metals that seep into the water table will be raised in a cheer to health at mealtimes and be emptied into pots to boil potatoes and collards, into spinach soups and tomato rice, sending many to early graves.

On our way to the river park, we stroll by more shops, their windows pasted with death notices, where people purchase their weekly lucky numbers. There are many lotteries to gamble on, and one to avoid. The heights of industrial wealth did not save one of the richest men in the country. He succumbed to cancer and is now residing in the same graveyard as his workers.

Tonight, in bed, after the three books I must read you and the three more stories I must dream up about the wilds of Africa or Canada, I turn off the lamplight and you fall unusually silent. The meditative chant from the stereo muffles, although does not block out, the pounding high heels of the woman above us, the loud TV commercials from the family of six next door. The more pleasant, repetitive harmonic trance attempts to shield the unpredictable rat-a-tat on tile, the bellowing motorbikes, and bass of car stereos soon to arrive at the pastry shop below to detonate your dreams.

"Are we also going to die, Papá?"

"Yes, we will, Koah. Everything and everyone dies."

"When will we die?"

"I don't know the answer, Koah. You don't have to worry until the day your bones move so slowly a spider will find time to build its cobweb in your hair."

You stare at me, puzzled.

I wink. "Most people die when they are old, very old. You have many years to live."

"But when are we going to die, Papá?" You do not blink.

"Not for a long time."

"Tell me a number, Papá. I need to know a number. Pleeeease."

There is nothing left to say. I hug you and let you feel the warmth of the living. It is not long before you fall asleep. You talk in your slumber, cry and moan and wake up, startled by the visitors in your dreams.

At sunrise, before I can kiss and hug you good morning, you wake up with a mission.

"I want to see Grandma's papá and mamã."

At the river, we take advantage of the fast-moving current to race acorns or oak leaves tossed over the weir. This is a race left to chance and the forces of nature; we cheer our boats from shore and wish them luck on their whirl-winding journey. The sun climbs high, and we seek shade by the watermill that, in my childhood, ground corn into meal. Against the cool granite steps, leaning on a bluer-than-sky door, we lay out a picnic of cornbread, green olives, and sheep's cheese. Every hour the bell tolls in the distance and lifts our gaze to the blue-tiled church towers by the cemetery.

In the afternoon, satiated, you step through the ten-metre-high wrought-iron gate into the fenced cemetery grounds. You halt. The many crosses, the vast landscape of white and grey marble glint in the sun. The speckled crucifixes on tombstones tower above you and multiply as far as your eye can see.

Worry empties your gaze before you turn to me. "Why do so many people die, Papá?"

"To give room to the young in this world, Koah."

You become pensive. We walk in the oldest part of the cemetery, and I gravitate to the right, toward the bottom path. You stop again.

"Why do they trap dead people under such heavy sheets of stone?"

Your hand runs on a smooth marble memorial.

I had never thought of it. I invent a reason.

"Maybe they want to make sure no animals will try to dig them up."

You look around. "What animals?"

"I don't know. Falcons, cats, dogs?" I shrug to emphasize the mystery.

Your head tilts in that please-give-me-a-break way, as if to say "I'm not that little or that stupid."

"No, you don't know." You sigh.

I smile a little less and shrug less confidently this time.

We walk the narrow grid of perpendicular lines separating the graves. The cemetery has tripled in size since my childhood. I am lost amid the hundreds and hundreds of coffin-long plots in this marbled sea, watched over by winged angels, Our Ladies, and crucified Jesuses. I pause at the gravestones brightened by fresh flowers.

"This way." You lead, resolutely.

I am puzzled at what drives you, since this is the first time you have entered this or any graveyard. I identify the double mottled-grey slat that marks where the earth now snuggles my grandparents. My three maternal great-aunts lie beside them. The marble glistens from yesterday's rain. The misty engraved sepia picture of your great-grandmother Maria Teresa shows her friendly smile. Beneath, two dates: 3 April 1915–11 May 1958. Your great-grandfather Manuel Maria's photo (18 April 1916–31 July 1982) shows the grieving face and dulled eyes I remember through his living days, a face he wore after the premature death of his great love. I am reminded that I, too, followed the family tradition of being born in April.

Every November first, this cemetery fills with families in black, remembering their departed. Only flowers brighten the grounds, for the mood cannot be brightened. Why November? Why the first? November guarantees skies at their darkest. The night overruns the day; the fog and the rain blanket the sun. Thousands of candles braid their smoke to the sky. This was a dreaded day in the annual calendar of my childhood, for its forced stillness and imposed silence, an unwanted rehearsal for death. I would be trapped within the gates of quiet, forced to stillness before the grave. I was expected to pray for the souls of ancestors I had never met. The prayers seemed belated in my child's mind.

Sitting on the grave, you inspect the sepia photos, run your hand over the smooth stone. I am hoping this moment becomes a type of meeting: that which is possible to accomplish across the fault of time. Or from the gathering of those dispersed molecules beneath your feet, now glued together only by stories in your memory.

"Where are Vovó's grandparents?"

They used to rest steps away in the Matos's family chapel bordering the old graveyard. However, even death is expanding its territory, and the tripled area of the graveyard shows that luxury real estate for the dead returns a profitable investment. The chapel, built by the wealthier branch of the family four generations back, has been sold, and the relocated remains of our far-gone ancestors have become nameless refugees beneath my grandparents' bones in our humbler family plot.

Soon, you wish to move onward among this sea of stone and stillness. I lead you on a visit to other relatives from the last century, and I tell you their stories and how we are related in the family tree. You listen.

After the graveyard visit, death has again bitten your mind, and you will now be weeks in its company. You interrupt our reading of a bedtime book.

"I'll never bury anything dead."

I raise my eyebrows.

"If I bury their bodies, I'll never see them again. I want to keep on seeing the dead."

A few minutes later, reading the second book, you ask me why Fox was not moving in the story.

"He was old and had lived all the dreams he imagined for his life."

"Why did he have to go dead?"

"Everything dies. The body just gets old and stops working."

You snuggle closer. "You and I are going to die." I detect in your voice a mixture of apprehension, sadness, and acceptance that makes my heart limp.

"Koah, you do not have to worry. You're four."

Your concern is palpable as you bring your face closer and stare into mine.

"Papá, you're old." Your eyes widen in sudden alarm. "You're going to die. What will we do then?" In your gaze, the existential anguish of our human condition settles. For a second, I am wordless. You stare, sensing I am struggling for an answer.

"I am older than you, yet not very, very mouldy yet. We still have dreams to live together, Koah. You want us to visit Africa and the lions. You want to learn to ride a bicycle, to read books all by yourself." This shift to our shared dreams calms your mind and hushes your anxiety, although in your eyes the issue is not settled. Perhaps it never will be. Many religions will pitch their philosophies, their particular answers to this question and attempt to enlist you in their ranks of believers. It will not be easy to resist joining a consensual belief system with its collective comforting shields, rather than living the questions, relishing the mysteries that may never be solved. The choice to live in the eye of doubt's tornado requires an inner strength, a strong sense of roots, and a fulfilling emotional network of affection to anchor and prevent aimless drifting.

The ache of losses to come is already a reality for your sensitive spirit. I cannot spare you the devastation you will experience, yet I am at a loss to stop you from worrying about that which is not yet here. As a father, I am tempted to deliver an answer. I believe I should have answers and be able to lift that burden from you. I do not know where this belief was born.

At bedtime, I instinctively shift from tales of polar bears and orcas gliding through their fantastic underwater adventures to stories of your grandmother Micas and grandfather Agosto in their courtship years, as well as to inherited family stories of your great-great-grandparents and the great-great-aunts and great-great-uncles you will never hug, whose calloused farming hands you will never feel caressing your strawberry cheeks.

I had imagined that living in Portugal for five months would allow us a daily conviviality with your grandparents, with the beehive of cousins, great-aunts, and great-uncles. Equally important is the visit we are making to the dead, resurrecting them through stories and perpetuating their existence for yet another generation. Stories flow at every mealtime among the extended family, a cocktail of generations reminiscing about the slower times when the world was always a smiley place. Anecdotes I have not heard surface alongside those I know. This is a land where third cousins make trips from nearby Porto and faraway Lisbon solely to meet you and your sister. This is a family tree that stands strong despite the oaks shaved off the hills. These are cousins whose roots remain here because their beginnings, still in oral memory, took hold in our valleys and hills. The soil that nourished their first steps will never be erased because the stories will not be forgotten for at least three generations. Your great-uncle Manuel, driving in from Aveiro after work, carrying gifts and a heart full of willingness to play with you and your sister, will not be forgotten for generations.

Great-uncle Manuel lost his mother at your present age of four. In those slower times, work stopped in the fields and people watched the funeral procession pass. As a child of eight, I remember those processions and participating in one, representing my family, overwhelmed by the wailing mother who was burying her eight-day-old girl.

Days before his mother died of stomach cancer, Manuel was sent to another family's house to be cared for. On a Monday afternoon, Manuel stood on a stone wall, watching a funeral procession pass, unaware that half his childhood and half his heart were slipping away beneath his eyes. He did not shed a tear. How could he shed a tear for what he did not know he had lost? That night, he was chaperoned back home to the new emptiness of the kitchen by his nineteen-year-old brother, José Maria. His father, Manuel, told him his mother had gone to live with the angels. The youngest of four, Manuel again did not cry. No one cried. The death and the loss were wrapped in silence, leaving each island of grief to digest its own terrors. Your grandmother Micas, seventeen, returned home from the city of Porto, abandoning her path toward an English university degree in order to look after the family. Her future was forever disrupted. Months later, she showed her brother Manuel a picture of their mother and asked if he knew who that was. He nodded in recognition. When pressed to voice his mother's name, Manuel said he recognized her and was not going to say aloud who she was. Young Manuel had lost the company of his mother even in his mind.

In last century's Portuguese culture, the recently dead were washed and dressed at home by family and remained overnight under the eye of loved ones. It was a vigil that did not let the living sleep. The open casket allowed the community a last goodbye. In my family, the children were kept away, as if adults could shelter them from the flesh's ultimate destination. As a teen, I was offered the option of looking at my grandfather's corpse and saying a last goodbye. I bailed. When I was twenty-five on a visit to Portugal, my paternal grandmother, Clotilde, died. I had seen her the previous day, on Christmas Eve, when she had devoured an entire chicken by herself. In the funeral procession, I carried the weight of many deaths as a pallbearer.

Amid the visit to the cemetery and my reflections on mortality, unbeknownst to me, death had already brushed my heart from a distance. Its bleeding had begun across the planet by the Pacific shores, but I had not yet heard its echo travelling on the Atlantic waves.

Late one afternoon, opening my laptop, news of my first love arrived on a pure white screen etched in black. The woman who had changed my life's trajectory from Portugal to Canada, so many years ago, had died by suicide.

Within seconds, you sensed the weight of sadness filling the apartment; you found me staring at the green hills.

"You are sad, Papá."

I nod.

You hold my face, pressing my cheeks between your palms. You do not know what is making me sad, yet you understand that pain is salty and burns any wound.

"Papá, you need to think of things that make you happier."

"That is wise, Koah."

Unlike other times when you claim my hand and pull me along to help with your Lego constructions, this time you leave without a sound.

Only three days before we left Victoria on this sojourn, Ginny had visited us from Alberta and talked to you in Portuguese. This touching moment rekindled a language she had not used in decades, from the time we had lived in these hills and in the medieval university town of Coimbra. It was because of her that you and I met, son. In this intricate web of life, we are all connected and affect each other's journeys through the miracles of synchronous meeting. Ginny wove our paths together by shifting my future to Canada. This occurred well before a succession of crossroads brought me to meet your mother and to invent you and your sister from our flesh. It was through Ginny that I learned to esteem the nation you were born in, where I chose to stay, despite the end of that relationship. It was through her that I learned to make snow angels, splash in glacier-fed Rocky Mountain lakes, and paddle the moonlike prairie badlands where one day I want to canoe with you, Amari, and your mother, Heather.

You and your mother and sister are the only ones who hold and hug my pain, catching my streaming tears with your kisses. My Cambra family encourages me to move on and be strong, keeping themselves at arm's length. What I would expect from a general encouraging a soldier to erase his feelings and march onward to death. The encouragement is well meant. My family is also in shock. Their hearts are bewildered. This is a time when the discomfort of grief, the pain of loss, are feared and their masking encouraged. Grief has been transformed into a disease to be medicated. your grandparents, great-uncles, and great-aunts have often been on sleeping pills to muffle their anxieties. I can understand the appeal of switching off the darkness: for relief, for survival, for the promise of peace.

Without such medications, I cannot sleep for a week, and in the night, I jump from bed in breath-stopping jolts of panic at the streaming images of my life with Ginny in this valley. For days, weeks, and months, the grief will return unannounced, the way it came the first time. It fills my heart to the brim, overflowing in beads of sadness, making a garland of sorrow around my eyes. Grief refuses to be silenced, and so it should.

At the dining table, staring at the untouched soup bowl, I want you to see the colour of mourning in my eyes. Mourning is a spiritual muscle that must carry me through the many sorrows that will cross my path. The heartache of Ginny's death is a new companion, an unexpected marriage for the rest of my living memory. Part of me has died in and with Ginny. The intimate memories of our life together are for me to carry alone from today onward or until I commit them to story. Hers is my first death in Canada. This is the first of many yet to come, if I am lucky enough to live long. I have lived in Canada anticipating the nightmare of waking up to a phone call summoning me to Portugal. Instead, the twists of life delivered me the reverse.

Although I am not religious, I am touched by my mother's gesture of requesting a special mass celebrated in Ginny's name. I learn then there are many ways of attempting to touch, even for those who cannot embrace.

Grief requires slowness. It requires a willingness to experience the live ripping of my guard. I must nurture the skill of patience, strengthen the muscle of grieving, endure touching the fire of annihilation without being incinerated by pain. I welcome the lifeline of your small hand nesting into mine, encouraging the letting go of me, the sinking, while my heart is at its most fragile, as it needs to be in order to touch the depths of who I am.

Our family of four was woven closer by Ginny's death, as it reminded us of the care we must carry in every word, and in every season.

Tonight you do not want the bedtime stories to end. When I turn the light off, you hold my hand more tightly and press your face against mine.

"Don't go, Papá."

I close my eyes and pretend to fall asleep.

I hope that as usual you will find your dreams within minutes, collapsing after a day of leaping over garden walls, street bollards, and any obstacle that crossed your limitless will—an energy spilling into the world and prompting your slightly older cousins Tomás and Simão to ask what you were "on." I whispered, "Love and passion for living."

Tonight I underestimate your attunement to my heart. As I attempt to move away, you dig your fingers into my palms. My eyes remain shut. Your breathing tells me you are keeping watch over me.

Tonight you do not fall asleep. I wait. I wait an eternity. Three hours later, you remain awake. My frustrated voice rises in the dark.

"Koah, it's kindergarten tomorrow. You must rest."

In my next breath, I regret it.

"I am afraid something is going to get you, Papá."

I tighten my hand, and you snuggle closer.

"Something dark, Papá."

I smell it. A deep creeping shadow perches on my shoulder, ready to swallow me. It is my inevitable grave waiting to seal me in its dark mantle. I turn the lamp back on. It illuminates your bright hazel eyes. I know I'll be shaking this shadow off my back and kicking it down the street for as long as I have the strength to hold my head above ground and remain gazing at your eyes.

the day nothing
happened

Standing beside me, leaning your head against my hip, you gaze at the surrounding Cambra hills. The ragged tree peaks tinge the high-horizon green. The flowering gorse paints a logged slope yellow. Your great-aunt Fernanda points to the tallest point. "Over there." She squints, and her straightened finger bridges the distance, bringing the peak to alight on her maroon fingernail. "It's a magnificent view of the valley. Beyond, you also glimpse the ocean, Koah. And when the westerly blows, it brings us the scent of the Atlantic brine."

The ease with which my gaze climbs the slope reminds me of any far range contemplation of landscape; from a place of stillness, at a distance, the lemony gorse is one more colour beautifying this living postcard that is the northern hills of Portugal. Unseen are the loose stones on uneven clayish ground, rutted by erosion, that unsettle our footing and could bring us down to experience the nitty-gritty of the hill on our skin.

The breezy Sunday afternoon has lifted the lead clouds over the peaks to offer us a dry opening after the earlier showers.

"We'll take you there."

Your great-aunt Fernanda invites us for a walk in the wood parcel she inherited from your great-grandfather Matos. Despite your immense affection for your cousins, when offered to choose between watching their afternoon game of roller hockey or this spontaneous walk in the woods, you do not hesitate in your answer.

A ten-minute ride in a Jeep transports us inside the charming postcard. We soon near the peak where, earlier, our gaze landed without a drop of sweat. After a week caged in your classroom, the wait for an end to the zigzag climb on the steep narrow road seems tolerable for the promise in sight. Excited, you jitter. "The trees are so close, like in Canada. There are forests here too." Your eyes twinkle, and you bring your shoulders close to your ears. The double dimple in your cheek deepens when you grin this widely. I do not wish to sadden you with memories you could not possibly have. Now these are hills of farmed eucalyptus, shaved off every ten years for pulp, not the pine and oak of my time.

Through the occasional opening in the treeline, as the road climbs to Our Lady of Good Health sanctuary, and along the granite cliffs, we glimpse the ocean in the distance. A trick of the eyes makes the ocean appear to sit above us. I prop you onto my lap, offer you the height to free your curious gaze out the window. We leave the asphalt road and cross large puddles that want to be lakes in the tire-chewed clay. We must stop. It is too steep even for a Jeep.

The door opens, and you are already in mid-jump, running along the rutted and impassable access road. Your arms stretch to the sky, and I know you feel at home.

This is a trip without *be careful*s and you glow. Even I, having been reimmersed in these ancient warnings during this extended stay, find myself wanting to deliver such warnings and require a conscious stirring of my awareness to use positive language. Instead of warning you, I attempt to bring you into focus and awareness, drawing attention to the varied terrain around you. It is not because you are a child. Adults also suffer from single-minded focus, especially when excited or disappeared in our minds. "Koah, please pay attention to the uneven ground and the roots." Before I finish my words you have tripped on the slope of loose stones and embraced the ground. The overlooked landscape details brought their existence to your attention. Now, you know them a little more deeply in the flesh. The sharp gorse prickles also meet your tender flesh, delivering you a song of pain as needles perforate your long sleeves and find your skin. Gorse is fierce in making itself known. You are learning that even beauty may sting, a reminder that you are a vessel whose blood may spill. As you roll up your sleeves, the writing on the skin resembles your stick-people drawings. I bring my face closer to yours to examine the damage. Your upper lip will grow a little fatter for a few hours.

More times on this walk, and during the course of your life, you will forget the roots, the ruts, and the deadfall again. For now, you hand me the scraped palm to blow the pain as far away as possible from the height of the moment. If possible, as far as the ocean in the horizon.

We carry onward on the trail. I rip a fallen eucalyptus leaf in half and let its blood sap exhale. You bring your nose close to my palm.

"Hmmm..."

"We use this eucalyptus oil to clear our lungs when we're congested, Koah."

I pick up a thin strip of bark from the ground. Your great-uncle Zé's smile stretches the map of all his wrinkles on his tall forehead. He understands what I am about to do. In his youth, and also mine, a time when toys and diversions were homemade and invented, we made windmill sails from eucalyptus bark. Two short strips of bark resemble an airplane helix, and we decorated them with the juice of blackberries, growing in the nearby brambles when in season. I raced on the trails, the motion prompting the helices to move, lifting off in my imagination.

Your great-uncle offers his help. He knows which curl and shape of eucalyptus bark to choose, knows the ideal dryness to make the blades move in a suave rotation. I watch and look deeper into a task that appeared to be easy in my childhood. You observe the slits that Ti Zé makes by pressing down his thick fingernails where one helix will cross over the other. His wide thick-veined hands inspect the ground for a straight smooth twig to become the blade's axle. Soon, you run down the hill and grin. The helices pick up speed and spin as in your grandfather's de Havilland aviation tales.

We arrive at your great-aunt Fernanda's thin strip of property that runs steeply downslope. To our eyes, the hill is just one and whole.

"Eucalyptus is our God's gift. Every ten years, they earn us a paycheque."

It takes ten years for a eucalyptus plantation to deliver a wood-lot owner the latest model of a laptop or SUV, depending on the property size. I understand the temptation. A pine forest will

watch children baptize their own children before the pulp industry would call trees mature, a euphemism for blade ready.

A spring bubbles from a side slope before it gains a wider body
in a stone-lined pool. This is the only place where I have seen the
moss that once carpeted these hills. In your great-aunt's youth,
this valley was considered the Switzerland of Portugal for its
enchanted hilly greenery and black-and-white cows dotting the
pastures—a time before the poisonous eucalyptus roots expanded
their newly conquered kingdom and, voracious in their thirst,
dried the hills, killing the indigenous vegetation that had dared
to also seek a drink. The tourist brochures still attempt to convince
visitors that the greenery remains. As for the cows, the rare tourist
is expected to imagine them.

We return, driving to the valley bottom by the east slope to check
on word from a neighbour that great-uncle Manuel's property
has flooded along the flatlands. The Moscoso floodwaters have
climbed to the fields and washed out a property-dividing wall.

We park on the muddy road before the swamped fields. The
water-filled ruts, as wide as the vehicle, force the four of us to leap
and tiptoe along narrow edges, a ballet blended with an awkward
hopscotch, to reach the fields of flattened river-combed rye grasses.
Forty metres away, loud and innocent, the small river sings as if
it never jumped course to explore other destinations within sight.
The stone wall will have to wait until summer for adequate repair.
There is nothing to be done, except to marvel at the will and might
of rivers that on occasion leave their carved-out destinies and surprise humans.

We file back into the Jeep to return home. The winter sun is no
longer visible above the hills.

A week later, free from Sunday roller hockey league, your cousins Tomás and Simão, together with their parents, join us on another excursion into the woods, alongside your great-uncle Zé and great-aunt Fernanda. In order to assess repair costs, the quest includes photo-documenting the rain and flood damage to the web of irrigation channels.

We stand beside two SUVs deciding how to accommodate and transport everybody.

"Can we? Can we?" the three of you plead.

Your grins reflect your anticipated incursion into forbidden territory, as you lobby in unison to pile in the vehicle's cargo space. Sitting on the carpeted floor, the ride promises to be bumpier without seatbelts, pressed in with the cousins, and therefore more thrilling. I understand. It is more fun to break road rules. You all climb in. The loud thump of the hatch door seals you inside. Your aunt Marina and uncle Filipe follow us in their SUV.

Sometimes you giggle, sometimes you shriek after a bump or a tighter curve throws your bodies into each other in a domino tumble. Laughter fills the vehicle. I exchange a complicit smile with your great-aunt Fernanda and great-uncle Zé. We roll down the windows as we pass the police station. A policeman waves; we wave back. It is a small town. This is the fun of breaking rules and being a little out of control in a world of increasing controls. Your great childhood pleasures will be remembered in these moments, a simple ride setting aside the expected map of everyday patterns.

We reach a hilltop, drive through a village built on the lip of a ravine. The Jeep follows a narrow road between houses, leaving one finger of wiggle room on each side of the already tucked-in side mirrors. The road continues past the village and along the edge of the cliff. On my side, I glance out the window for the reassurance of ground. I see none, only the deep ravine and the thread of a river far at the bottom. At times, I wonder whether the clay road edge could collapse and roll us off this cliff. I anticipate the guilt I would carry were I to survive, as I glance toward you, oblivious to the danger and lost in laughter. About you travelling in the cargo space, what would I tell your mother and sister, at this moment enjoying their long afternoon nap?

The logging road continues, dropping into a steeper zig-zag descent. We stop and park past the last isolated house. The moment the hatch door opens, you run to the nearest tree and attempt to climb it. At the bottom of the ravine, a hundred metres below, a clear creek snakes through the landscape of stone and eucalyptus. Near the creek's embankment, the standing skeleton of an old farmhouse glows. Its ochre crumbling stones glint in the sun, reflecting a past thriving farm life by these waters.

"Let's see how many wild boars we spot today," I say.

You and Tomás cheer and race down the trail. Simão quietly walks to his mother's side at the tail of the group. He holds her hand. Your bravery, Koah, comes from not knowing exactly what a wild boar is and what it could do to you if you were charged. The likelihood of meeting one face to face is remoter than this remote trail.

The steep zigzag descent encourages our speed. After the first switchback, we stop to examine the ground, chewed up from rooting wild boars, their tracks distinguishable in the lake of mud.

"You were not joking," Simão mumbles.

"They must be near," you say, wriggling your hands and grinning.

"Maybe we don't have to really go down there today," suggests Simão, pointing with his nose to the creek and pulling your aunt Marina's hand back up the trail.

The eerie silence highlights the strong sun and the collective huffing and puffing. Soon, we hear steps following us from a distance. The woman from the last house in the village catches up and would like to join our excursion. She enjoys walking in the woods, but not alone. "There is never anyone else here," she adds.

"Have you ever seen a boar?" Simão asks.

"Only from my kitchen window but never while on foot. They don't like running into people."

Simão's impish grin returns. His feet lose weight, and he leaves his mother's hand to join you and Tomás leading the group. Soon, we learn that this woman, in her late thirties, grew up here and emigrated to France as a teen. She returned while her husband remains abroad working. They have been purchasing much of these woods surrounding the village, believing land is a much wiser holding than paper money or the intangible numbers accumulating in a bank.

"This is paper I can touch every day and see growing." For evidence, she touches a resilient eucalyptus sapling growing from a stump next to the trail. We are crossing a clear-cut area, recently logged. I don't ask but imagine it could be hers. "Of course, woods can burn down. If they do, well, it won't be long until they grow again." In financial lingo, this might be called the dividends of the earth. "If your money vanishes in a financial wildfire, it is gone for good. Ask Lehman Brothers, or the next financial wildfire victim yet to come."

I smile. This is the wise ancient attachment to land, reflecting a belief about the true source of prosperity and financial security.

"Wealth only exists where our feet can stand and call it their own," she concludes.

You have disappeared around the next switchback, and when I spot the blur of your yellow T-shirt again, you could be a gigantic bee busily seeking the disappeared flowers. I find you off the trail with Tomás, inspecting a hollow den under tree roots made larger by the logging trail erosion.

"Could this be a wild boar's den?" Tomás asks.

"It could, but they seem to be out for Sunday church."

You stare at me along with your cousins, attempting to decipher the seriousness of my statement.

After fifteen minutes, we arrive at the canyon's bottom where the dense vegetation offers shade in the vibrant greens of alder and oak. The waters have filled the metre-and-a-half-deep irrigation channel with boulders and tree debris. In one channel segment, a family of six mustard-yellow frogs pile atop each other in a puddle. We hop from boulder to boulder, approaching the fast-moving creek. Many fiddlehead tufts, taller than you, decorate the rocky shoreline. I explain to the woman who has joined us that in Canada, and elsewhere, these curled green tips are a prized delicacy. Everyone shrivels their noses. I whisper to the fiddleheads, "You are safe."

While I photograph the flood damage, you toss large stones into the water, generating loud splashes or detonations of stone on stone. Simão and Tomás join you. You climb and slip, trip and leap. You clasp a vine, slide down a slope. This is your gym, your preferred playground equipment were you given the choice of residing here. We walk to the mouth of the irrigation channel and find a boulder several times my body mass, blocking and jamming the large metal door of the levee. Only dynamite will remove it. Your great-uncle Zé sighs; his large prominent hazel eyes widen to take in the whole picture. He anticipates an insurmountable amount of physical labour to return this irrigation channel to its intended function. Heavy machinery cannot reach this valley bottom.

The fast torrent colliding with the boulder sprays creek water, creates an aerial ballet of droplet configurations that mesmerizes. We stare in silence at the ever-changing landscape of the current and the whispers of moisture painting the air, changing the picture before our eyes from moment to moment.

On our return, we stroll past the side trail leading back into the torrid sun and the bare hill. We wish we could remain in the lush cool bottom that travels beside the creek, a universe of moss-carpeted boulders serenaded by the turquoise rushing water. We walk on the wide stone wall of the irrigation channel. If we carry on for three kilometres along this channel, we will reach the channel segment that passes near your school, where we walk every day to race our leaf boats. Your great-uncle Zé offers to pick us up on the other side of the hill. You are eager. I turn around despite your disappointment. I know your desires loom larger than the ability of your body. On the other hand, my own desires to continue have already reversed, a condition of aging, accepting limitations. My instinct soon proves to be accurate. I have to carry you on my shoulders for a portion of the ascent back up the hill.

Simão walks limberly and more relaxed. He and Tomás catch up and request a break. We wait for the others. I set you on the ground since we are not far from our destination.

"We aren't going to find wild boars, are we?" Simão asks with a satisfied grin. His pink tongue shows through the missing front tooth lost in a golf club swing accident.

"Can't believe you missed them, Simão. They were soooo loud."

"Where?" Simão stops. Fingers curled into his hands, his dark brown eyes bounce in every direction, seeking the danger. He frowns and scans the clear-cut landscape surrounding us. You and Tomás scan the woods for a last ray of hope.

"Three of them, in fact," I say, laughing, tapping the three heads around me with my index finger.

"Argh!" You all snort in unison and chase me up the hill amid laughter. A last burst of energy is still stored in your small bodies.

We say goodbye to the woman carrying a lush bouquet of fern fronds and wild flowers collected from the creek's edge to beautify her dining room table where she will eat with her daughter and no husband.

"My daughter will complain," she confides. "She says they are more beautiful where they belong in the wild."

You and I nod to each other. We agree that many a time we have been guilty of acting on that same temptation. After all, you love flowers and ask to smell hers.

You spot the Jeep and cheer, anticipating the return-trip adventure in the cargo space. The hatch door opens. You are first, jumping in for another journey of laughter and collisions with your cousins.

Today we did not encounter the wild boars, the Jeep did not slide down the ravine to the river, and no one was left behind on the climb. The day unfolded without mounting anxiety or a climbing curve of tension released in dramatic denouement. The parallel plots we encountered had been abandoned and now grew wild with ferns and flowers. Today you and your cousins were among the trees, the frogs, and the singing river, arriving at the vehicle bursting with grins and the most brilliant, happy faces.

Today nothing happened.

walls

Where do the children play?
— CAT STEVENS

Your blond hair and aqua-blue striped smock leap to my lap smelling of your teacher's jasmine perfume. This scent has lingered from a classroom where the teacher's consoling kisses, lap, and embraces mingle with classmates' shoves and kicks, elbowing and cries, scars and broken bones. When you run into my arms for a hug, I return to engaged fatherhood and hold my breath for the daily menu of injuries. There have been two black eyes, three cut lips from being shoved onto the cement floor, two or three cranial egg bumps—a rooster's crest as they are called in Portugal, after the male dominance fights in the chicken coops.

"How did you cut your lip, Koah?"

"I fell on the cement."

"What happened?"

"I fell by myself."

I raise my eyebrows in surprise.

"I thought I felt someone push me over. The kid chasing me said I just tripped and fell. His friend told the teacher that's what happened. So I must have tripped." You shrug.

There is not yet a malicious bone in you. I bite my lip and swallow my anger as I reach for the first aid kit in my fanny pack. We are still applying Traumeel on the black and purple skin around your cheekbone after the pencil jab to your face, and now we will add red to the colour palette while I clean that cut and that sadness from your face.

Every day you arrive showing a different cut, bruise, or scrape, and I turn my face so you do not see mine. The playground is a play-pound, a collision course or a human bumper-car track holding forty unwound kids running on a cement strip, twelve by four metres, meeting the obstacle course of benches, pillars, a lemon tree, a see-saw, and a large yellow and red cement train. A space that in Victoria would not be fit for a canine obedience class.

Grasping the ledge above your head, toes scraping the rough cement wall falling in patches, you hoist your body onto the playground divider and cling to the long metal bars. Your gaze searches for your cousins on the adjacent elementary school grounds.

"Be careful," a grandmother warns, unable to contain herself in the face of my complicit silence. You do not hear her. Many children have already learned to muffle out those two words from their vocabulary so as to live a semblance of a childhood. It occurs to me I cannot recall a child telling another to be careful of their adventures.

I turn to the grandmother, smile, and assure her, "Koah is an acrobat in training."

She frowns.

I do not wish for words to function as a vocal whip or short leash that declares you incapable of weighing risk and gaining invaluable experience from your successes and failures. Allowed to test your limits in our Victoria playgrounds, you have moved beyond your years in strength and agility. At twenty months, your tiny hands clenched a crossbar above your head, and your feet slid across a second crossbar well above my reach. I held my breath. You held yours too. Those slippery pipes rose well outside my intervention—as you well intended. Your grin awaited me on the other side.

Much earlier on your adventures at the Beacon Hill playground, I also remember lunging to catch you in the air, as one would spring for a baseball, whirled from a knee-high merry-go-round; this, after you unexpectedly decided to stand up amid the other kids while in full merry spin. Nine months of luck crystallized in that moment. All gasps, all eyes following your airborne trajectory through space, and I, on one leg, stretching my torso and arms to catch you in my hands. I did not laugh that time. The silence touched everyone. It may be true these misadventures were the reason for my first white hairs. The fears were mine and not yours. I contained them since they belonged to me alone.

I am cognizant of the risks while I watch you dangling from the wall in the school playground. Luck is a mysterious star, as I was reminded, growing up in this Macinhata neighbourhood where I was dissuaded from climbing trees because, doors away, my mother's childhood friend was spending her life in bed after breaking her spine falling from a fig tree.

Yet those adventures have built your resilience, independence, and confidence. They offer you the skills to evaluate risk, to problem-solve in preparation for life's steeper ascents. Knowing your appetite for thrill, I wonder if you will decide to climb the heights of Sagarmatha with its high death ratio. Will I feel guilt upon remembering the early training grounds that conditioned your adrenaline-addicted brain?

In this school playground, despite the disapproving grandmother's head shake, my role is to monitor your adventures from a distance, ensuring that the risks and mistakes are not deadly. I am not here to shelter you from every ache and mistake. I am here to introduce a few challenges, pains, and risks in a safe training ground, well before life throws you the mean ones, those without mercy and support.

You kneel and stir dust into a puddle of yesterday's rain. Another child follows you with his gaze, and his grandmother fidgets, pulling him along a little more firmly toward the gate. You are unaware of your lightning-rod quality, attracting the gaze of caregivers and the curiosity of other children who wish to experience your freedom. I join you in dirtying my hands and trousers, despite the disapproving glares of parents and grandparents, fretting over the dust and mud, the sneeze-inducing winter sunshine, the shiver-generating rain, and the climbing children.

From farms to wood mills, from cheese and butter production to furniture factories, this was a valley that lived from the riches of its fecund soil. This is now a town of "Be carefuls" and "Don't dirty your clothes." Later this afternoon, you will kneel on the fields among the goats and their droppings, poking sticks into the gopher holes as the curious goats peek over your head. Great-aunt

Fernanda, trimming osier shoots, and great-uncle Zé, lifting a trellis, will both relish the sight.

We disrupt the after-school pattern by introducing the sin of spontaneity. We stay in the playground after the bell to do what kindergarten children could have been doing most of the day.

"Who wants to run laps with me? Um, dois, três. Ready. Set. Go."

Soon you enlist three classmates. They are eager to escape the routine: exchanging the school's set of four walls for the home's, where they will stare at the babysitting screen. You set up laps around the inner perimeter of the walled playground, invent games of poking twigs through the metal mesh in the play equipment. This is not a town where hired nannies pick up children. Every adult arriving to collect a child is a blood relation. The impatient grandparents and parents are caught between wanting to please their children, understanding their desire and right to play, and the pressing routines keeping the rolling train of the day in its tracks.

I join you and your friends in your laps on the dirt around the two swings and a slide in the elementary kids' playground. I am the only one over a metre high participating in your runs, the stick game, and racing down the slide with a carousel of kids; we are a circus speed act daring not to collide. The other adults are the shepherds holding on to stillness, an arm's length power that prevents them from entering our fast-moving child's universe. The *be careful*s rain on us at predictable intervals, mimicking the unsounded tick-tock from the church-tower clock not far away.

We linger in the playground for your lap races. Soon, a child from your class trips on a stone and falls. Crying erupts. You hurry over.

The sound of pain stresses you. You are the first to console him. The other children laugh at the fall. It is a common response here. The tumble becomes the proof the fearful grandmother has been waiting for: that the safest existence for a child is in stasis. She admonishes her grandson for the fall that was almost his, and determined to trick his impending fate, she pulls him homeward by the wrist. I, too, understand the appeal of wanting to see stillness in a child's play. It would shelter my parental anxiety, protect me from the discomfort of hearing a piercing cry. A fall would instead call me to witness, turning me into the consoling arms where pain empties itself.

In a few weeks, I will see you laughing at a classmate being tripped and falling. Other parents will shrug and say, "Kids for you."

Despite these new models of interaction, you remain an affectionate child, kissing or hugging boys and girls alike.

Earlier, as you walked out from your class, hand in hand with Gabriel, a mother exclaimed, "Koah is sooo sweet."

"The kids love him very much," added another mother.

Not all are happy to see you collect attention or even enjoy your ease to share hugs or kisses. To some, your need to connect and be close is perceived as an unbearable asphyxiation. It is true. You are an intense child and lean near to gaze at them in the eye. For those children who already cannot hold their gaze with another, closeness is a torturous moment.

The next day, as I walk into your classroom, you proudly wave a drawing of me and point to *Pai* written in your unsteady handwriting. Green twiggy legs spring from my head, and I am missing arms. Some days I do feel that disjointed. It is an accurate psychological portrait.

After only a handful of days in school, you write your name and mine; soon your sister's and mother's names will also appear. You have learned to hold a coloured pencil and draw with more precision, while mastering the sharp elbowing to delineate the space you need to exist at a table. There are forty kids pressed on the squared benches singing, and you show the behavioural signs detected in chickens crowded in factory cages: aggression and a quick jab for your space.

In this class, there are no conceptual bubbles around the body to teach personal space and autonomy, as you learned in Victoria. If a bubble, conceptual or otherwise, did exist in your consciousness, that bubble became target practice for children pushing your boundaries, testing the permissible in a race to discover who would pop more. Your bubble burst in the first week of school when you arrived home black-eyed, after another child poked you with a pencil and barely missed your pupil.

You rush to retrieve your green tweed hat from the clothes rack and meet me at the doorway, tripping on the low wooden bench. The fall on the tile floor, the crack of the knee, prompt me to leap inside. You rise to your feet unusually slowly and limp toward me, biting your lip to contain the pain. You cry only when you find my arms around you. Then you cuddle in my lap.

"Bad, bad bench," the teacher's assistant says, smacks the wooden bench, making the stern, angry face she also uses to admonish the children.

Bewildered at her response, you slow down your crying, wipe one eye on your sleeve, then say, "I just tripped."

In her intended lighthearted offering of solidarity, you are being taught to blame something else other than your distraction for your fall. Distraction happens to everyone. You are being encouraged to take your frustration out on something outside yourself in order to feel better, in this case with aggression. I remember identical reactions from adults to my own falls decades earlier. Well-intentioned remarks are passed down from generation to generation, imprinting a relationship with the world and others. This is how you learn the unwritten rules of interaction; this is how you learn to respond to your emotions. Unaware, you are being taught to blame.

On the walk home, you are quiet. Your usual tumble of words and flaming smile are absent.

"In Portugal, teachers hit children," you tell me.

I stop, ask for more information.

"I slapped teacher Isabel's bum as she was slapping the bum of my friend, Gabriel."

"I am sorry, Koah. In Victoria, a teacher cannot slap a child. You know that."

You nod.

I crouch to offer a hug. You lean into my chest.

"The teachers shout angrily too."

I see the consternation in your face. After a few days, your voice will rise in pitch and in aggression. You are learning in this kindergarten that aggressive behaviour gets results. That is why you see cousins, uncles, or aunts talking over and interrupting each other. They are not listening to one another. They are not learning. Many are still hungry for attention and love. You are discovering emotional scarcity and strategies to win when competing with forty children for the attention of three adults. This is children partly raising each other and childcare workers doing their best within an inhumane system. Everyone has been set up to lose. The children lose the most.

This morning, you resist sliding into your clothes; then at breakfast, you pick at your porridge. This is your strategy to block every step toward being ready for school.

"I don't like oats." You push the bowl aside, showing an emphatic expression I do not recognize.

I raise my eyebrows. Until today you cherished your porridge, never complaining.

You have become a picky eater in the last couple of days. I understand. Food is your last bastion of control. It is the domain in which you may arrive at your desires in the power imbalance with parents and the world. The battle for autonomy has been transferred to food and clothing choices, a resistance that could grow through the years into perpetual teenage rebellion if I do not offer you autonomy and respect.

When the knock on the apartment door arrives for you to join your cousins on their way to school, you throw your blue striped smock on the ground and refuse to wear it. I have not seen you this upset. For the first time in your life, you have experienced the powerlessness most young children live through when forced away from daily life with their parents before being ready.

The excitement of attending school with your cousins was tainted by the first week's bullying, and you have realized that daily kindergarten is not a brief adventure. You are being placed in a painful, unsafe setting. You question your trust in me to watch out for you, the job of any parent. You are correct. Three adults in your classroom cannot oversee the power imbalances among forty children at play. I have passed on the baton of daily responsibility in raising you, and the education system has not met my expectations.

You rebel, engaging your might to draw attention to your needs. You have been cornered against more than a wall, experiencing little control over the unfolding of your day, forced to learn resignation and to follow the Monopoly squares of daily living as others also learn the rules and abide by them. The only learning game for children in this town is this game of attending school. You were raised with far more choices and do not easily slide into unquestioning obedience, which is itself a type of violence. Even joining your cousins in their morning journey to school, three musketeers wearing satchels and raincoats, boarding a wheeled gasoline-powered horse, was bait that did not mitigate the rest of the day to follow.

You and other living beings will adapt to lost freedom and autonomy, as any neurotic animal in a zoo or human prisoner will attest. Confined to a newly imposed reality, you, the imprisoned, will exercise any possible degree of autonomy. In small or large gestures, you have expressed your resistance, arm-wrestling for control so as not to completely annihilate your spirit, self-worth, and respect. And so you stand your ground and say no. You do not want to go.

"School is boring," you complain. "I don't want to go back."

After the first week's excitement, you now face the repetitious doldrums that prepare a worker for the industrial world.

Your anger is doubled. You are being removed from your family. Your sister, father, and mother will stay home for the joys and frictions and annoyances of togetherness. You much prefer love with the occasional flares of irritation with your sister or parents to the claims that you will be learning new things. You know you can learn a storm of new things anywhere, including in the bosom of the family. You are being herded to the corral and you smell it.

At home with us until the age of four, you had been living in a historical past resembling the childhood seen in agrarian times amid the family. I like to think also that you have been living in the saner future we are rebuilding after large-scale industrialization bombed out the family economy. A future you will be helping to create since you have tasted its gifts. One day, once again, a family may opt to work from home, and such choice will be seen as a feasible, desirable, and wholesome way to raise a child. Imagine the *melros* flying their chicks away from the nest to be raised in a factory, the moment they hatch from the egg. That is what day-cares and schools do. Wait, that is what chicken batteries do to feed the industrial system. When children spend most of their waking hours away from parents, placed in learning institutions, we should not be surprised when those same children place their aging parents in old-age institutions to die on their own.

Reluctantly, you accept the return to school after negotiating your terms. Today I will pick you up a little earlier. I oblige. I remind you that you come home for lunch every day for an hour and a half break. All in all, you are in school three and a half hours in the morning and one and a half in the afternoon. In Canada, most preschool children are absent from their families for six straight hours, much longer if attending pre- and after-school care. You seem to appreciate your partial luck of a midday parental connection in Portugal. Home-schooling or unschooling are concepts yet to be practised here.

Before we part for the morning, we hug. We blow kisses as we say goodbye, and you walk into class. You turn back.

"Pick me up in this tiny a time," you tell me with a fierce, angry face. I imagine you assemble such an expression to depict authority, as you perceive it. The curl of your index finger nesting in the thumb leaves a miniscule hollow through which you look at me. It is apropos. You are a tiny *I* at the end of a time tunnel, the tiny light at the end of a dark and narrow school day that separates us. You do not want to disappear into the black hole.

I tease you. "No, never that tiny." I show you a gap even tinier. You smile, then make one even narrower.

That is the infinitesimal time it will take to cross that school-time divide. It translates to *I'll see you again after your solo journey into your first underworld.*

At home, after school, you admonish Amari for not following the rules of a game you have made up and are playing together. School has taught you not only to follow rules but also to enforce them. Later at dinner, you explain that a new girl arrived in class and that she is doing everything wrong: talking when she should not, standing when she ought to sit, sitting when she ought to stand. That is how you felt only weeks ago.

"I showed her the right way to do things," you say, nodding your head, proud and serious.

After dinner, you reach for your schoolbag and show us the official class pictures you had forgotten inside. You are the only person wearing a blueberry tuque. Amid forty children, two teachers and one assistant, posing in five rows on the entrance steps, you stand apart from your peers, uneasily gazing sideways into the camera. In your portrait, you wear a navy-blue pile jacket and appear stiff, serious, as if you have been commanded into this pose. Your vovô Agosto says you look like a German general. He has been on the front lines of a few wars and must recognize a battle unfolding in your eyes.

I see sadness as never before.

When I pick you up today, your teacher assures me you are not unhappy during your time in school. It is true. Your default disposition is contentment, even when your inner world faces turmoil. You are a joyful soul. After the first week, your teacher says you have become aggressive and are first to prompt classmates to break rules. It is understandable. You are a fast learner. Your independent spirit will not be tamed. It will resist and fight back, applying the same aggressive behaviours that have been used to crush you. My work as a father is to teach you that we do not join wars if we want to change the world. We model a different way of being. Not easy when you feel continuously under attack. You have begun to draw your boundaries and show your growl, fist raised in a kind of capoeira defence, holding a protective arm across your face. You will not be an easy target. You have learned to defend your territory.

"Give me space," I hear you say to another classmate in the playground. He does not understand the shape of words in your accent. He presses on, kicks your piled pebbles and twigs. You growl and show your teeth. These words that request space become your Portuguese refrain, a shield that is insufficient to stop the onslaught of changes that crush your known world.

During the first few school days, you learned to survive in your new environment by standing behind the shield that is your teacher, clasping the hem of her blue striped smock. You cling to her dedication. Her love for the children is palpable. Your teacher cuddles, embraces, and assuages. Her exhaustion is visible, her commitment magnificent. She and the other teachers invest extra hours creating intricate costumes for Christmas, Carnival and patron saint day parades. These festivities bring you and your classmates to the Cambra streets to be cherished by the entire community. Children recite five-minute-long poems or song sequences, believing they are already little Broadway stars, adorable performers displaying their tricks. The intentions are pure and commendable; the consequences of people-pleasing and identity through performance are complex and not all applaudable.

We are playing in the living room before bedtime. Amari finds a lost tiny coin on the tiled floor where you were playing with your piggybank. She pops the coin in her mouth.

I catch the motion through the corner of my eye and shout, "Coin out of mouth, Amari!" The voice comes out loud and strong.

You sister's body recoils, her hand also, and brings the coin out of her mouth. Immediately I whisk it away. Amari shudders in silence, about to cry. You walk over to console her. She, like you, is sensitive to admonishments. Unlike you, she is still tender about raised voices and will bring her head to the floor, cover it with her hands as an injured bird might cover her whole body with her wings.

"It is all right, Amari." You embrace and kiss her. Then you turn to me. "Paulo, you don't need to shout at Amari. You can just tell her not to put the coin in her mouth . . . nicely."

"You are so right, Koah. I was scared Amari would choke. I will remember next time. Thank you for letting me know. It was a very nice tone you used."

In a moment, the tempest passes and I embrace Amari who is still unsure about me. She tilts up her head from under her hands to search my face for clues of a weather change from the earlier stern stance.

Both of you carry on playing together. I smile. I, too, continue to carry the schooling of shouting from this culture. It is clear you have learned and heard it from me before. I am relieved in my fears that this time, in this culture and school, would sweep you down a one-way street without return. This time in Portugal will not change you forever. We are fortunate we have your mother who came from a much kinder, softer family and cultural background and who rarely raises her voice. You have been exposed to alternative models, and your preference is apparent. She, too, has been my schooling.

Three months into your school days in the valley, you stopped the recently acquired habit of pushing your sister and kicking her without reason; poking your finger into her face in a new karate move of recess school torture was a side effect of the unspoken curriculum. Since the Easter break started, you have relaxed, and miraculously the rough play has vanished. Could it be that spending your days at home has eased your need to aggressively defend your space?

"*Podes dar-me espaço?*"

In perfect Portuguese, while we play-wrestle on the sofa, you ask me if I could give you space and step back a little. I smile. This is yet another language you have now become fluent in. It allows you to overcome frustration by telling people exactly what you need. Few may imagine what it is like to be tossed into a crowded schoolroom where your needs may not have been heard, let alone understood due to a new language barrier. Now, I cherish the return to your jovial self: you are relaxed, not under attack.

At bedtime, you ask me to massage your back while I tell you a story about a stallion growing wings to lift him above harm's way. You tell me what you like and what you do not like in my touch; you guide me to the places where you want your tense back muscles eased. You fall asleep, once more trusting that the world will see and hear you.

It has taken you three months in school to adapt to the different rhythms and expectations in this unique culture. Only weeks into your journey, I lay awake at night listening to the barking of a dog intermingle with the clip-clopping of the woman in the apartment above, wondering whether it was time to flee this Cambra valley as I had done in my teenage years. Now, halfway through our family adventure, I wish we would stay a little longer. It is my hope that the seeds of this sojourn will continue to grow so we can reap the fruit in our future visits.

In your first foray into full-time kindergarten, you learned herd discipline. Self-discipline is a much more important skill to learn. People have been conditioned to follow others and to bow to authority. Internal discipline is difficult to attain but essential to steer your path against invisible crosswinds and tricky undercurrents.

On top of the wall, wearing a wide grin, one arm clasping the playground fence, you lean into space, sweeping your free hand as if you were flying. The grandparents and parents know you now and have given up on their *be careful*s. You have learned to climb the psychological walls in this school and to stand higher above the given landscape. You have moved through anxiety and anger, tension and aggression, learned the rules of the school game, and do not let them define you. You know you have broader choices and wider horizons in which to pursue your dreams, unlike other children here. Your classmates hug and kiss you as in the very beginning. The ones who are not so inclined have stopped picking on you, realizing you will stand your ground if necessary, and that tenderness and shyness are not the same as weakness. Tenderness is a strength you share with those children who have never been touched by its softness.

invisible wealth

We only become what we are by the radical and deep-seated refusal of that which others have made of us.
—JEAN-PAUL SARTRE

"The wealthy Canadians enjoying their proceeds," your kindergarten teacher quips on her way home for the weekend after class as I sit on the cement steps in the sun, enjoying a rest from playground races with your schoolmates and you.

In many eyes, Koah, our family displays affluence in our availability to care for and play with you and Amari. We embody good fortune by living in this Cambra valley for over five months without appearing obliged to work at a daily scheduled job. We share freely of our clock when many believe that time is money in this new world of racing economics, and few people find empty hours for their families and children, let alone for friends.

Behind our time-wealth appearance lies a constellation of unorthodox choices and priorities that make our bountiful time resemble a magic trick once believed to be reserved for magnates and royalty. The arithmetic of independence—or freedom from clock bondage, as I am keen to say—is broadly presumed to be a consequence of inheriting a treasure chest of gold coins or winning the lottery. That simplistic conclusion—time is money—becomes true only to those who believe or allow it to be true. Your mother, Heather, and I have discarded the notion of ladder-climbing careers for more meaningful rewards, including time to be. Time can be created. Time can be carved out and given the shape we envision, the way we shape an hourglass sand sculpture on a tide-flooded beach.

Alongside kale and arugula, in the mild Victoria climate, our family cultivates time. It is our best cottage *industry*. We do not carve out the hours from our days to watch sport matches, T V series, soap operas, or to play computer games. Time is finite, and as precious as a fig softening in our Fernwood backyard. We make time to read aloud together, to splatter in the mud, and eat meals as an endangered four-headed family dinosaur.

Those who believe our Canadian family to be affluent do not imagine that we have rented our home in Canada to pay for this journey, as we do every year to finance visits to our Cambra family. Internet-discovered strangers use our green-paint-peeling rickety Geo from the '90s, sleep on our creaky, salvaged mattresses, and occasionally polka-dot our bedsheets with scarlet nail polish or break a porcelain family heirloom. This sacrilegious invasion would not be an acceptable financing option to most in this valley.

Nevertheless, your mother and I chose not to pursue race-to-the-top careers, chose not to be chained to an all-or-nothing expectation of a sixty-hour workweek in exchange for a forty-hour cheque and strict schedules, in order to climb to an elusive professional Shangri-la. The financial perks would not replace time lost from your childhood. Despite the appearance of doing nothing since I do not commute 9 to 5, the writing of this book occurred in spurts or after midnight when you, and most people, curled into your dreams. My work is the invisible labour of any writer cast away from the respectable visibility of a factory, office, or academic roof. I have learned to juggle numbers, bills, and to become a financial magician at the oddest hour. The hybrid skills of creative artists committed to practising their devalued art, while helping to feed the family, border on miracle-making. We are CEOs of resourcefulness, which the planet tolerates better than CEOs of finite resources.

By heeding the insights of mythology, literature, and philosophy that have mapped the trappings of human fears for millennia, and by studying those reflecting on the pitfalls of flocking behaviour, your mother and I have learned to chart an alternative path for our clan. We have avoided the reactive, predictable urge toward the blinding sun or safe haven. In my previous life as a buffalo stampeding in fear toward the cliff of my future crushed bones, I charged ahead, busily following others, not stopping to ponder the essential question: To have or to be?

Our family abundance is plainly visible and appreciated by you and your schoolmates as we make the time to run around in the playground after class. Our treasure chest is in our hearts being free from the lassoes of busyness. On Father's Day, when Momma asked what you appreciate about me, you did not hesitate: "Playing with you, Papá." You prefer our time together to candy bribes on a growing mountain of toys that I could not have bought you to compensate for my absence.

It is Saturday morning. We accompany your aunt Marina to the small nearby city of São João da Madeira where an oversized mall imported from America now colonizes the ancient cornfields. The traffic resembles marching ants guided by the scent of the sweet post-Christmas discount sales. This is a shopping and entertainment mecca for the surrounding small towns.

Once inside the glittering mall, you stare at the metal shape-shifting steps unfolding, folding. Ahead, the ground is moving. You hesitate, then clutch my hand and leap. This is your first escalator ride and you gape at the mechanics, the effortless progression of bodies. Before arriving at the top, you are already sold on it. You ask to travel up and down in a loopy carousel of unending trips. It is addictive for an impressionable mind of four revering the magic displayed by our adult-constructed world.

The dimple in your cheek deepens, giving away the depth of your joy. This escalator loop could have continued for hours, and until I became loopy myself, were I not to intervene. This is my role as a father: to lift you out of traps that take you nowhere, so that one day you will recall the pattern and remember to extricate yourself from sticky compulsions. Soon I will tell you those escalators, time after time, only deliver you to the same landscape. They move at a pre-set pace; you are locked in the sardine school alongside other restless bodies. The moment you have stepped on, it is impossible to jump off until it has delivered you to a designed destination of aromatic fried everything, or a shop window flashing pink Barbies. You better hope the ride is short. You better hope you never take the wrong escalator. Time moves faster than the fastest escalator. While standing still on the steps that move forward on your behalf, you become a mere observer of a world passing by. You have been taken for a ride.

When the escalator delivers you to the second level, and we see the entrance to the movie theatre for your first cinema experience, your aunt Marina is already waiting, ready to introduce you to the troupe of animal detectives in *Zootopia*.

I stroll away, perusing the endless store windows on this floor. Then I return and select a red plastic table in the food court that offers a view of the escalator. I open an underweight novel. When I raise my eyes from the page, I do not see any smiles on the people streaming toward the downward ride where it all began. Their shopped-out arms strain under the weight of oversized bags; their heavy eyelids are semi-closed for inventory and budget rebalancing.

From my red plastic table, my gaze trails a surging tide of bodies entering a nearby kiosk to place their lotto, lottery, and *futebol* bets. Still scratching five *raspadinha* tickets, a woman in a fluorescent-pink track suit and matching runners walks out as if already resigned to her slim chances of winning. This is the busiest doorway in the mall. In my mind, I attempt to measure the employment time I have saved by not gambling for forty years. I further entertain this mind game and tally four decades of not buying beer, smokes, sport event tickets, gum, cable TV and cellphone subscriptions, first-run movie tickets, marijuana, Coke and coke, Pepsi, wine, bar tabs, and Mars bars. I conclude that my *Homo sapiens* diet, free of hydrocarbonated drinks and gambling, has saved me four years of wage-earning obligations.

I do enjoy games of relative chance and low odds, but the only lotteries I win represent the smallest literary grant awards that prompt me to celebrate in jubilation. I become a virtual billionaire for six months, indulged to dive recklessly into my word compulsions.

My gaze is drawn to a hiccup among the flowing bodies at the mouth of the escalator. The human stream pools, spreads. An elderly man, leaning on a cane, ponders the step onto the rolling descent. He wobbles, succeeds. Momentarily free of the perpetual limp from his knee, he sighs, relieved. The pool of people soon drains out.

I am reminded that there was not a single escalator in the Cambra valley when I escaped in my late teens. I gladly strolled away myself. Soon after, in my twenties, I reached a few heights of my own. I climbed the mountain passes of the Rockies and the Himalayas. In Nepal, inside stone-piled walls, the Tibetan or the Nepalese families shared everything they possessed: their bowl of rice and their abundant smiles. There was no visible wardrobe inside their abodes, and they wore the same clothes for a week. They laughed freely.

Dazed from the collision with brightness after two hours in the theatre's booming darkness, you stroll alongside me, uninterested in store windows. But soon your gaze catches something unusual. Your steps halt at the sight of naked mannequins. Their bareness prompts you to comment, "They will catch a cold."

You are four years old and have yet to wear new clothes purchased by us. I have not bought myself new clothes in decades. In my life, I have not acquired a single piece of new furniture—not even the cheap IKEA variety. By many financial measures, we should qualify as poor. It is a poverty no one in our family experiences. Our fridge is full of kale, carrots, and potatoes.

On Monday, when you button up your blue smock in preparation for another school day, the garment reveals your cousin
Tomás's name embroidered over your heart. From your clothes and
shoes to your Lego, nearly everything you own has been inherited
from your cousins in Cambra or friends in Canada, or received
as birthday and Christmas gifts. Amari's clothes have mostly been
inherited from your Myanmar-Brazilian friends. Like your parents,
you do not know or care for brand names. The excitement of your
new-to-you clothes grows from their histories.

This morning on our way to the mall, you stepped out of the
Cambra apartment beaming with pride. You announced to your
grandmother Micas that the snug turquoise raincoat over your
shoulder had belonged to Simão. You feel connected to your
clothes in the way you feel connected to people, Koah. Clothes
map a continuum of affections. A scarlet pullover from Tomás is
received as an act of his care, an understanding that he is willing to
share a cherished outer skin. It is a privilege to make it your own.

Amari, two steps behind you on Heather's arms, giggles, elated
by the vibrant reds of her tropical-Brazilian frilled dress. Gestures,
combined with one-syllable exclamations, convey her delight to
her grandmother Micas; the dress belonged to her best friend.
If garment brands are not inferred as status symbols, and their
price stickers are not a reflection of your individual worth, no
stigma becomes entangled in the weave. Values and morals are
embedded in every story offered to you. What I underline by my
excitement and cherishing actions, Koah, is what you will hold
relevant, and so it will stand until the day you are confronted with
another mainstream story. The Sony or Levi's, Adidas or Apple
behemoths engage their megaphones of persuasion to draw you
into their consumptive world view. They will claim more than

a little something from you. They want you to marry them for life. On that day, you must ponder your choices, find your own story around goods, time, and freedom to be...or be bound by the chase for an externally constructed desire—usually costly, always unending—for goods that are not so good for you.

All these time-wealth equations—no TV, reused clothes, and no predictable career destination—are directly related to the freedom to choose, the freedom for time. In the calculus of hours, minutes, and seconds, sharing and frugality are the invisible modifiers. In my erratic, diverse salaried life as a waiter, health-food-store cashier, NGO office coordinator, short-lived labourer, and caretaker, I have succeeded in working less than a twenty-five-hour week, but well over eighty at everything else I cherished, income-generating or not. Your mother has also preferred the shorter workweek for most of her paid stints.

Tonight, before the pastry shop closes, without shame or remorse, I will walk down the staircase of the apartment building to buy its half-price pastries and bread to bring you and Amari the rice muffin you relish.

At the end of the trip, I know your grandmother Micas will ask me what I purchased at the mall. I will say, "Nothing." She will look incredulous. In the same way, I might say I visited Fátima and did not return displaying the pope's smile on a keychain to remind me and everybody that I two-stepped on that Catholic sacred ground. On my first few visits from Canada, I would arrive in my old room to find newly bought T-shirts, shorts, trousers, jacket, and once a long sea-green winter coat. I would ask your grandmother Micas to ricochet them to the stores or donate the lot. I truly did not need them.

"But you're wearing the same clothes from the last four visits," she would exclaim in horror.

"I like them. They're comfy."

I preferred to inherit the old long black coat from your grand-father Agosto, which I still wear to this day. Grandfather took the new one.

Since before you were born, we have not eaten out at a restaurant in Canada, and it's even longer since we have sat in a repertoire movie theatre. I am not missing out. It is my choice to cultivate time and togetherness around a muddy puddle and to make bea-ver dams in the garden, instead of raising expenses. Our fun is homemade with grit.

We have lived as a family not split by the gospel of the indus-trial revolution: the more you consume, the wealthier you are. Instead you have grown accustomed to expecting my presence in your daily living. At my doorless office–living room desk, you have access to me any time you desire. I have learned to write with inter-ruptions, and many at that. Your mother takes on the occasional month-long teaching contract. Meals and snack times unfold in the company of both your parents and sister. You have grown accustomed to the carousel of roommates sharing our house to help with bills and income, even from a time before your birth.

It is true. We benefit from the overflowing abundance in our urban societies. The range of our choices relies on living in a pros-perous, throwaway Western country, where we can live off the surplus: from rusty, sidewalk-discarded bicycles to refurbished laptops to thrown-away high chairs and day-old rye bread.

We also benefit from a well-off society that pays decent wages when we choose to work. We have never depended on social safety nets or unemployment insurance. Frugality and sharing are the seeds we cultivate in order to harvest the time we cherish.

I am not blind to our contextual privileges. Our ancestors on both sides of the family started with nothing to their names, and their sacrifices delivered improvements to every successive generation. In the Vermoim hills, your grandfather Agosto shared a sardine among five siblings on the festive day when there was a sardine to share. I, on the other hand, have never experienced the continuous stabbing of hunger hollowing out the belly. Your grandparents arrived at the middle-class finish line with time to spare. We enjoy the privilege of choice. We enjoy the privilege of a noisy place to lay our sleepy heads in this Cambra valley. We enjoy advantages inherited from your grandparents and their grandparents' choices in a constellation of family focused priorities, sacrificing themselves for future generations. Even today, your grandfather Agosto denies himself the purchase of a daily newspaper. Instead, he walks to the cellar and picks a newspaper or Sunday magazine from the bottom of the two-year-old recycling pile inherited from your great-uncle Zé. He reads for the love of reading the news. I offered to pay for a daily subscription. "They are just words to entertain me," grandfather Agosto explains. "I enjoy reading the news. Even old news ends up sounding fresh after years have passed," he concludes. He also resisted my suggestion to replace the broken lawn chair, which is missing its padding, where he reads the newspapers, the tilt stuck in a perpetual unmoveable angle. Avô Agosto has taken his breadwinning responsibility beyond his future grave, as most Portuguese men of his generation do. He deprives himself of "luxuries" such as a newspaper, in order that his children and grandchildren inherit his savings and be assured an easier future. That forward-thinking care for the well-being of his bloodline lives within me as a vision true to our family bond. Not one engineered by Marlboro, Malibu, Mercedes, nor one to invite the invention of infant and youth needs concocted by Nestlé, Netflix, or Nike.

Alone, I do not have the power to reallocate collective resources, now directed to building monstrous sport stadiums or missiles, and channel them to end hunger, house the homeless, heal the ailing, or offer alternative learning environments. I do not have the executive power to invest in the wellness of all children and families by enacting a public policy that provides a long-term option to be at home raising young children, following what many European countries already offer. For the time being, I can practise my support of that vision by opting to live as a parent at home for the first several years of your and Amari's lives.

That opening quip from your kindergarten teacher—"The wealthy Canadians enjoying their proceeds"—indicates that Cambra valley parents may understandably envy our free time and leisure, our slow living and availability. Ironically, in what counts most, we are wealthier than most middle-class families and likely more fortunate, in a better way, than many of the bank-fat. Few billionaires may be counted among the time affluent. Preservation and expansion of riches is time-consuming and often removes parents from the company of their children, who are mostly raised in private childcare.

Meanwhile, your mother and I seek the margins of existence, not unlike the coyotes retreating to the partial freedoms found in the remaining and less disturbed natural spaces, on the edges of Western Canadian cities. Neither coyotes nor our family are interested in living between zoo fences or in any safe institution—though, on occasion, our animal neighbours benefit from raiding garbage bins or bountiful gardens. On the margins of the predominant values of being and living, we find the breathing space of our humanness. In pockets of wilderness, in nature or in the city, we and the coyotes may still find ourselves less pressured by the profit motive and by its socially mandated policies.

Our family is not ruled by pre-cut life designs, not ruled by destination traps that await us, when half-asleep from tireless overworking and stepping out of bed to enter the daily, rolling walkways of labour. We have opened up our life choices by avoiding fast currents guaranteed to sweep our days along predictable patterns. For this insidious ailment of stress, stemming from the inhuman pace of people's days, and the breakdown of extended family clusters, the common "wisdom" proposes a destressing medicine that adds more consumption to many lives: a Riviera cruise, a Club Med holiday, a Walt Disney destination. Today even fun carries its own high cost. Lifestyle is the lengthy indenture of people's 9 to 5 working days.

In the margins, you will find more room to manoeuvre. Every time I choose a road that deviates from the consumer highway, I am empowered to believe in the change that can be achieved one step at a time. I am trying my best to carve an unconventional path until my last breath. Resignation to things as they are, and becoming an accomplice by my inaction, would be a living death. Active change inspires our family spirit and illuminates a world of possibilities.

the colours
of happiness

And the need to win
Drains him of power
—**CHUANG TZU**

Your uncle Filipe repeats the mantra "Portoooo, Portoooo, Portoooo" in a low incantatory voice as he pushes your one-year-old sister, Amari, on the swing in your grandparents' yard. She stares at him with a quizzical face. He prompts her to repeat the words. She focuses on his lips. He does not see me observing from the portico outside the kitchen, and only when he hears my footsteps approaching does he stop abruptly, pretending to be chatting with her.

Your uncle is not teaching Amari geography by naming the second-largest city in Portugal. He is teaching her to chant for his *futebol* club, his first love. I smile. He is on a mission to convert his Canadian niece to cheer for his team. He does it undercover to later pretend children arrive at team allegiance out of divine inspiration, a story that mimics Paul the Apostle and his sudden conversion when struck by divine light. That enlightenment parallels his often-recounted story of how his two boys, your cousins Tomás and Simão, arrived in the Porto fold, as if they ultimately had a choice in the matter. Futebol team allegiance is an enclave of belief that runs in families and is passed from father to child, as if one were passing on the secret to happiness and the meaning of life.

Welcome to futebol, the most popular unofficial religion in Portugal, and possibly on the European continent, although it goes by the less conspicuous name of sport.

On your first visit to Portugal, you are nine months old, and after picking us up from the airport, Uncle Filipe swerves into the first shopping mall on the outskirts of Porto.

"A quick, important stop," he says, casting an aura of mystery with the twinkle in his eye.

We wait, imagining he must have remembered an essential grocery delicacy still missing for our welcoming lunch in the valley.

Uncle Filipe returns shortly after, grinning from eye to ear.

"Koah, you need to arrive in style, showing off this beauty in your hands. You'll give our *seleção* good luck."

Your uncle reaches into a plastic bag and presents you with a red and green leather ball that you can barely grasp in your small palms. Your eyes sparkle at the bright colours, at its largeness.

The ball bounces from your lap and runs away from you, inviting a chase. Your mother and I have now acquired a new job as ball boys.

In the weeks ahead, despite your wobbly, learning steps, holding our hands, you spend hours kicking and chasing the green and red ball to our amusement and delight.

Your uncle Filipe's spontaneous gesture reveals a heartfelt welcome to the nation and the culture, signalling membership in the core of your uncle's life, and of many others in this country. It is his tribal welcome to futebol. If you are to be emotionally connected to the men in this family, you have just been shown the sport's iconic symbol. This is the initial piece of the altar. More paraphernalia may follow, from diapers to scarves, from key chains to wine brands in the colours and emblems of the "right" team.

On that first trip to Portugal, we land on the opening day of the European futebol championship and taste the fever in the air: green and red flags hang from windows and balconies, cars decorated with ribbons and flags honk, shuttling to and fro, while blaring the official team song. Cristiano Ronaldo posters now outnumber those of Jesus in cafés and barber shops.

Two weeks later, on the day of the semifinal against Spain, we stroll outside after dinner for an evening promenade, and the deserted streets offer a preview of an apocalyptic world. It is delightful to be the only family ambling along the streets enjoying the warm evening. The absence of noisy cars and motorbikes is notable. Inside the crowded cafés along the sidewalks, the nervous tension releases intermittently in what we guess is a near miss or a controversial referee call, as spectators surf the emotional swells of their adrenaline-drenched brains.

Later that night, the spectral silence and funereal faces exiting the cafés reveal the fate of their hopes. It will be a good night's sleep for us and for the rest of the country.

Around the lunch table at your grandparents', Ti Filipe, Ti Zé, and Grandfather Agosto's conversation settles on the usual futebol, their high-revving words invigorated by cornbread, olives, pickled lupini beans—all washed down with red wine.

"...so after the final whistle, we chased the referee, alongside storming fans with their umbrellas hacking and poking, sending the man to hospital with ten broken bones on his face." Your great-uncle Zé laughs, before adding, "He deserved more. The shameless crook."

Ti Zé and Ti Filipe exchange more stories of their days as earnest amateur footballers, recounting their glorious moments, or their mean, cunning plays ending in broken legs, torn Achilles, and black eyes.

You sit in the stroller, focused on the green and red ball perfuming the air with its leather breath of new. Somehow you bounce the ball from your lap to your foot three times, as if there were a magic string preventing it from falling. Your uncles and grandfather look in awe and hope. "The future Cristiano Ronaldo of Canada," says Ti Zé. "Koah sure has a great ring for a striker's name. You will be the first Canadian to play for Sporting."

Family mythologies and storytelling now build around futebol and team accomplishments. The clan bonds most tightly when wrapped in one jersey colour, framing its experience and collective memory. The lore of their past futebol achievement melds into their hopes for every son to progress a little further than they did, to achieve respect and immortality through the game.

"My great-grandfather was a staunch Porto supporter," your uncle Filipe says, tossing an olive into his mouth, spitting the pit and taking a sip of the wine.

How proud your uncle Filipe is that his team affiliation has been handed down from his forefathers; it would be an affront to the family tree were he to give his heart to a rival club. It would be unthinkable for his sons, Tomás or Simão, to wear an archrival jersey colour. This is not a trivial matter. The well-being of a father-and-son relationship rests on this tribal initiation in a stadium or before a TV screen surrounded by cheers, chants, and curses. Futebol is the rare bridge that leads fathers and sons to sit next to each other and share the same psychic space. Shoulder to shoulder before that TV screen or turf, in their *ohhhh*s and *ahhhh*s, in their yells and curses at referees or players, two generations share and communicate their joy and frustration. They touch elation in each cheered goal, travelling the same vibration, the same ecstasy, and so the men feel whole and connected. This is a relationship mediated by the chance and chaos of a game. It is not a relationship built on agency and purpose so as to build a new world together.

When the time comes, Uncle Filipe promises he will take you to the Estádio do Dragão in Porto, along with your cousins, for an initiation ritual into manhood. The aim is to bring you into the fold. He hopes that the adrenaline spilling from fifty thousand people chanting in the festive atmosphere of blue, that the elation brought by a scored goal, that the congregation of minds cheering will flood you with excitement and hook you for life, as it did his sons. This is a type of ecstasy pushed on impressionable minds, a promised gateway to quick happiness or misery in ninety minutes.

In the afternoon, Ti Zé offers you a Sporting cap, saying green is the best colour in the world, since it is the pigment of the earth.

Ti Filipe offers you a toy car with the colours and emblem of Porto. He extols the virtue of blue as the most important colour in life, for it is the hue of sky and water. An argument ensues between them about when the sky or the water are not truly blue but also green, and from the outside, this argument resembles that of children taunting one another. Puzzled, you stare at both, uninterested in either cap or car. You continue kicking your new ball.

The family contest is on to conquer your loyalty to their teams, just as the different religious faiths also battle for the souls of people. Today your uncles battle for your allegiance to their futebol knights galloping through stadium fields, yet those idols are nothing more than the adored slaves of our century, rewarded with a royal lifestyle. They are our new entertainment gladiators: bought, sold, and traded.

Four years later, it is 2016, and we are staying in the Cambra valley over the winter and spring. Upon our arrival from the airport, as every year, your cousins Tomás and Simão ask us what our futebol team is. You look at me, puzzled. I smile, tell them, "No team." They insist. They have not met a man in this valley who does not choose a side in the perpetual carousel of rivalries and teasing. When they insist on an answer—for they could not possibly relate to us in a void of tribal allegiances—this time with a wink, I say, "Valecambrense," the local team nobody cares about. Tomás and Simão shake their heads in disbelief and drop the matter for the day.

This first week back in the Cambra valley, we gather around towering cardboard boxes for the exciting task that you anticipate every year: rummaging through the treasure of shoes, shorts, trousers, coats, and sweaters that you are inheriting from your growing cousins. A trove you proudly try on as it means you are growing up, following in their footsteps, linked to family history. A gift our entire family is thankful to receive.

Declining the earnest offer from cousins Tomás and Simão of their Porto jerseys from younger years or the cap from your uncle Zé and vovô Agosto's rival futebol team is not without consequences. Your cousins bite their tongues, fall silent, and grow distant, eventually leaving the apartment.

It is an awkward moment for everyone, as are many ostensibly innocent moments that entail difficult and unique decisions. It is not only a jersey that I refused to let you slip on. I protected your identity from being reduced to tribal clans of irrational sports affiliations passed down from generation to generation with more fervour than ethical or moral principles. Blind devotion is an easy place to slide into as one might slide into a gang membership where belonging is attained by unquestioned allegiance.

Later that afternoon, we also decline the invitation to sit in a café, wrapped in a veil of cigarette smoke alongside Uncle Filipe and your cousins, where they will cheer players in a game. Our refusal may seem innocuous; however, not joining in such communion at the altar of futebol is an affront and affects the emotional foundation of family connection.

For the next few weeks, you are not invited to join them when they play a game in the park or on the video consoles at home, and since their time spent around those two activities is substantial, you have now lost a significant share of space and time to connect.

It is only March, but the fever already grows for another cycle of the UEFA European Championship in July, taking place in France. We will be back in Canada by the time futebol fever brings

Portugal to its pitch-high fervour with a cup win. You and I will miss the midnight congregation and the euphoria of your cousins and Uncle Filipe. They will drive around Cambra streets amid thousands, mostly boys and men, waving flags and honking, to celebrate a European title which the country has been dreaming of holding for decades.

This is a collective fulfilment that will boost the confidence of a small nation and its boys, despite low economic and social standards of well-being for the citizens. A high is a high, and people seek it to escape their depressing day-to-day realities, an addiction widening its targets. Futebol is the emotional drug of choice, and despite its highs and lows, for most, it is the best promise of hopes realized.

Tonight we walk to Ti Marina's apartment across the hallway.

"Let's offer company to the futebol widow, shall we?" I tell your aunt and add a teasing wink.

She frowns and wrinkles her freckled nose, half-serious. She is ironing clothes and partly watching a talent show on her wall screen. The women are not beside their men in the cafés. They remain home attending to the children, ironing next week's school and work garments, cleaning bathrooms and cooking. If childless, this is often their only time to themselves, so they secretly cherish it. I am yet to understand what women truly feel about their husbands' game obsession, which appears to override their attention to them. I wonder what else women feel, besides their resignation to the inevitability of this compulsively male-centred universe, their acceptance of the established order of the world. The women laugh off the futebol madness and step aside from interfering in the children's indoctrination when their own family-of-origin futebol tribes collide with their husbands'.

Tomás and Simão are outside the kitchen on the large terrace. You join in the chase, kicking the ball without purpose. The game is new to you, and you do not know or care for its rules. The exuberance of goal scoring you see in your cousin Simão, fist pumping in the air, is contagious and the feeling you are after. Soon enough you will understand the point of scoring, of being first, and will learn to want to win too. Simão enjoys dramatizing his moves on the field. He has already assimilated that futebol is as much about skill as it is about pretending, a game within a game. Fast and lean with his footwork, Simão fakes being tripped and claims a penalty after he has lost control of the ball. He is already a skilled player, not needing the tricks and cheats of the game, but he has learned that winning is more important than truth, and so he plays his well-learned deception card. It works often enough in this sport. But we do not fall for it. We do not indulge him. Simão becomes upset and refuses to play.

A cold wind blows, and we move inside to play foosball instead. You need to stand on tiptoe to reach the handles to twirl the players. You love scoring on yourself and celebrate to your cousins' despair. A goal is a goal in your count. I laugh. I let you score on our team. It is the celebration that matters. The goal is the excuse. I join you in scoring on ourselves, pretending it was an accident. This becomes incomprehensible to your cousins, who grow in desperation and frustration. The fine details in the equation of power and winning are still beyond your desire to master and achieve. The trickster in you is here to stay. I hope for very long.

The futebol obsession is crystallized in my childhood memory, where the intersection of madness and the game ensnared Moreirinha, a farm labourer, as he ferried back and forth from the fields, hauling fresh grass for the cattle in his corral. Blue tin cart overflowing with scentful grasses, Moreirinha grunted up the steep lane, never once stopping his loud play-by-play of the imaginary game unfolding in his mind. Passersby's greetings and short conversations were woven with the fast-paced dribbles of the players moving in his mind. The goals were relayed in a long, glorious *gooooollllllooooo* wail, lighting up his and every neighbour's face. I met him daily in your grandparents' lane, smelled his wafting of earth and manure, saw his trousers stiff and crinkly, held together by a hemp string, admired his days' old glistening stubble.

I maintained my distance from this mythical creature dwelling outside the expected bounds of social behaviour and predictability, even if he displayed perpetual contentment in his universe of oversized gestures and megaphone voice that mimicked the radio futebol announcers. Moreirinha's futebol team, Belenenses, which represented a Lisbon neighbourhood, had claimed one 1946 Primeira Liga championship to its record, making his love and allegiance to this improbable future champion the true verdict of his madness. For decades, people had been smiling and teasing, cajoling his insistence to cheer for a thirty-year-long losing team.

A fanatic's behaviour is entertaining and the source of endless laughs, making for a fine character in storytelling, be it on the page or screen. A fanatic's distorted passion appears comic, and at times even romantic. In art, these characters hold universal appeal since only their obsession is highlighted, and the viewer never has to live under their roof, or be impacted by the collateral consequences of their behaviours and beliefs: emotional and physical absence from family and children, the unpredictable pressure cooker brewing up their frustrations and anger to violence, their financial resources channelled away from the family fridge, or the emotional instability of their moods dependent on external results. Growing up in the Cambra valley, stories of men arriving home frustrated by their team's loss and taking out their frustrations on their wives were recounted with a smile of humour and inevitability.

On Sundays, the radios blared the play-by-play of futebol across the country. The men sat around café patios, listening as their emotions travelled the swells and dips of the game, eagerly waiting for their happiness to arrive in a long wail of a goal to blare from the mouth of the transistor, as if an angel were delivering the fate and fulfillment of their days. Some Sundays the angel delivered, in the names of divine messengers like Eusébio, Yazalde, or Gomes; other days, not.

Later on, as a result of widespread car ownership, wives joined their husbands parked in their Minis, Citroëns, and Peugeots along the main streets of each town. They exhausted their afternoons stationed under a boulevard tree, the wives knitting beside them, listening—or not—to the game on the car radio. To this day, on Sunday afternoons, your grandfather Agosto will head to the car or lounge on the sofa with a tucked-in earpiece, listening to his hometown Oliveirense team, whose second league games are not televised.

I am telling you this as a recovering footballic. At four, I collected potato beetles from the fields for sprint races in the corn-threshing patio; they raced in imaginary jerseys representing the three most popular futebol teams of Portugal. If my beetle did not race ahead in a straight path to the finish line, I had already learned to interfere with a supersonic index flick that transported the creature to victory, while I basked in the approving smile of my coach Ti Zé, always drilling and testing me for my faith in the team.

"And the best club in the world wins another," Uncle Zé congratulated me.

So you see, Koah, I had already been taught that winning must be accomplished at any cost. What mattered was winning, not sportsmanship. One could only enjoy a game if one wins. You have already experienced a flashback of me in your more intense cousin Simão, who becomes surly whenever he does not win. The winning obsession is shaping his personality and making him unpleasant company in any type of game. Simão was not born surly. The unrelenting incitement to race and eat his meal before his brother, to get into his morning clothes first, or finish his school work before any other has taught him that life is a race he must win, lest he be forgotten and invisible. That love and attention is a reward for winners only.

I liked the futebol that once was. I enjoyed playing the game semi-competitively in high school and recreationally until the age of seventeen. The town's coach remarked when I was fourteen that I was a natural talent and asked me to commit to more practice, to play the game more seriously. I declined, preferring to play for fun. I was headed for university, and being accepted was already competitive enough for my liking. Another talented player on our team committed. He made it to the national team.

I still enjoy kicking a ball around for fun. Not vicariously supporting the multibillion-dollar futebol business and the backdoor corruption that controls it. I enjoy the teamwork required to accomplish a goal, the silent communication between players who understand each other's minds better than their lovers', who anticipate their desires and intentions in the ball chase. I enjoy the intricate skill and beauty the game can display, with or without the object that resembles the world itself at my feet.

Today I would rather play a game in which a team is working toward a common goal and not facing another team whose objective is to be an obstacle and impede our accomplishment. There are other activities and games that hone collective skills without the adversarial aftermath; however, I was born in a town of few offerings, and futebol was the elected game among boys. In his childhood, your grandfather Agosto played futebol barefoot kicking balled socks, since real balls were a luxury during World War II. Many a time, without a ball to be had, I, too, played futebol tag with my friends. The human, representing the ball, had to be tagged before he darted between two stones serving as goal posts.

I spent most of the unscheduled hours of my childhood and youth playing that beautiful game on the street, in a clearing, or on a sandy beach while on holiday. It brought the neighbourhood's boys outside to be together with a common focus. I also played ringlet and hopscotch with the girls, often the only boy to do so.

As a teenager, I felt trapped in a sleepy town, waiting for the adolescent years to die in a hurry and for my leaving to arrive. Sundays, apart from morning church services, offered nothing more than trapping flies against shut windows. Every second week, the blaring accordion notes from the futebol stadium chased the frightened birds across the skies, jolting alive the village for a rowdy party. Once the game started, the roars of the crowd stirred the cats lounging in the sun, and the women stopped their domestic chores to receive the ecstasy from the crowd, united in their orgasmic scream. No church service could match that mighty choir.

Between the ages of ten to thirteen, before your grandparents inherited and renovated your great-grandparents' Matos home, we rented the main floor of a tiny white house, a stone's throw from the stadium. On Sunday afternoons, I jaywalked across two cornfields and hung around the entrance gate with the other boys until allowed in by the kind ticket collector, after promising we would be the loudest-cheering fans in the crowd of five hundred people.

Alongside the boys on my lane, I sprinted to the standing-room area behind the goal, climbed the two-and-a-half-metre-high brick wall, and perched on its ledge, leaning back against the high wire mesh that caught moon-bound penalty strikes. Only ten metres behind the goalkeeper, my friends and I enjoyed a perfect view of the entire field, avoiding the checkered obstacle of the barbed-wire fence that separated the fans from the players. Rain or shine, we relished our crow's nest, sitting well above the obstructing bodies of adults who stood below us, and the ear-piercing shrieks of the fishmonger harpooning obscenities at the referee.

During the week, I pored over my team's table and standings, or the anticipated calendar games. I read sports newspapers and followed the trading gossip, comparing stats, tossed in the emotional whirlwind like an autumn leaf rafting through a raging irrigation channel. Even after decades away from this weekly roller coaster, the mental branding of futebol from my childhood remains an emotional tattoo I cannot erase, although I have learned to ignore it.

My final disenchantment with the game arrived in the spring of 1985, when Italian Juventus fans were crushed to death, trapped against a wall and a high barbed-wire fence as the crowd fled from charging English Liverpool fans brandishing knives and throwing rocks. I watched the TV image zoom into the face of a middle-aged man pleading to the camera for help as the panicked crowd crushed him and many others against the fence. His face pleaded centimetres from mine. I, helpless to save him, wondered about the horror experienced by his children watching their father's demise while sitting in their living room.

Thirty-nine people died, and six hundred were injured. The youngest was eleven years old, and while thirty-nine bodies lay on the tarmac outside the stadium covered in Juventus flags, and while the helicopters shuttled the injured to hospitals, the UEFA officials, the players, and the fans carried on with the start of the game.

That was the last time I sat to watch a full game on TV. Many, many more people have since been murdered, victims of futebol's fanatic violence. The face of that Italian man, whose name I will never know, has lived with me ever since. His flailing arms, like the wings of a trapped bird trying to escape through the fence, are forever imprinted in my psyche.

Years earlier, at that same boyish age of eleven, I escaped a similar fate, compressed between adults pushing their way through a narrow stadium gate that had been closed to ticket holders in an oversold stadium. Standing behind my uncle Zé as he carried his toddler son on his shoulders and another son by his hand, I was crushed against bigger bodies, swept along in the human wave forcing its entry. For a few moments, compressed between bodies and unable to breathe, I panicked, fearing for my life, until the gate collapsed and the pressure eased. I had lost my uncle in the sweep of the crowd. Too small to see above the mass of standing bodies, I never glimpsed a player or a play in that game. I spent two hours sitting or kicking stones, waiting for time to pass and for my uncle to find me.

The effervescent mood on the streets is visible as most anticipate tonight's futebol match between rival cities will bring a roller coaster of emotions. This excitement travels as far back as the beginning of this sport in Portugal. T V coverage already seeps through every café window as patrons secure their seats near the large screens, despite the many hours until the referee's start whistle. The cameras zoom in on the arrival of each team's luxurious bus at the stadium, alternating shots of opposing claques chanting, blowing horns, beating drums, waving scarves. The thousands-strong claques are escorted by cordons of riot police herding them to each segregated area of the stadium. I cannot imagine you there among that deafening noise, that nervous and aggressive excitement. We stop in at the bakery and pastry shop beneath our apartment and buy fresh buns to accompany our fettuccine lunch. As usual, you choose pão da avó (grandmother's buns), a large sourdough bun whose soft dough you enjoy scooping out with the hook of your index finger. The bread is still steaming. You cannot wait to dig in. On the T V screen, an all-in-blue fan professes his love for his team, yells encouragement to his players, guesses the goal scorers with confidence, and assures viewers his team will win by a large margin. He kisses the emblem and swears club fidelity forever. An opposing fan props his head over the first and seizes the cone-shaped microphone to promise to walk out of the stadium on his knees if his team wins. He is already missing a tooth.

Dressing up for the part and chanting the team's anthem to become one with the whole may appear humorous and cute at your tender age of four. It mimics the initiation into any sect or gang of any denomination and affiliation. Yet people seem surprised by the rise of fan violence, the clashes, and the militaristic, gang-like behaviour. The recruitment message is insistent and aggressive, a campaign modelled after the missionary zeal of other spiritual tribalisms, a journey that cannot but end in antagonistic confrontations and a sense of separateness.

It is late December and warm. Your second cousins, Tiago and Joana, arrived this week from Brussels to spend Christmas in the valley. As usual during this holiday, they will drive three hours to Lisbon to watch their team's game. Tonight's match ends at 11:30 p.m., and they will drive back that same night. It is a quick and obligatory pilgrimage to Alvalade every time they are in the country. The excitement runs high before their departure as you and I stand in the yard, playing before we see them off. They want to take a group photo with their Sporting futebol clan in green and white striped jerseys, caps, and scarves. They ask us to join in. I decline. I say I am no longer a *sportinguista*. In Portugal, the word is a noun and an adjective to define identity as one defines a nationality.

Silence ensues as the mood of our cousins and great-uncle Zé shifts from incredulity to that of an unexpected joke, until it morphs into a deeper and more mortal seriousness. I have betrayed the Sporting nation.

"Do not say such a thing," our cousin Hugo says, waving his arm in dismissal. His friend cocks an ear. In his eyes, I detect a glimmer of hope. I have become a possible convert and there is no better banner recruitment than one who might trade faiths.

The green jersey photo is taken without us. You continue to play hide-and-seek in the yard, for now oblivious to the drama of belonging and not belonging.

The cousins begin singing the Sporting anthem, and the loud chorus draws your curiosity as you arrive holding a football in your hands.

"What are they singing?"

"A song that makes them believe in the same thing...or the same goal," I explain, smiling.

You scratch your head, puzzled. "Is that like being under a magic spell?"

"Kind of."

Your wild laugh rises into the sky as birds toss their songs in the trees. "Why don't you join me instead, Papá?"

I sprint after you, snatching the ball from your arms. I toss it toward you, giving the ball a sly spin. It bounces back to me. You screech, tricked again, and for a moment pretend to be mad, before we begin chasing the ball, holding onto our bellies in riotous laughter, lest the game runs away from us.

three pastries
and one appetizer

Bica e Bola de Berlim (Espresso and Berlin Ball Doughnut)

Dough:

50 g baking powder
350 ml milk
750 g flour
2 eggs
2 egg yolks

90 g sugar
70 g butter
1/2 lemon, zested
2 tablespoons of rum
Flour, oil, and sugar to please

Filling (makes 2 teacups):

1 egg
2 egg yolks
250 ml milk

40 g flour
75 g sugar

The metal chairs scrape on the tiled patio of the bakery opening for business beneath our apartment, waking the three of us at 6 a.m. This thundering shake reverberates through the bones of the building and in our own. The scent of baking and brewing seeps up through invisible veins and nearly makes me forgive the waking jolt, foreshadowing of the sugar and caffeine jolt soon to be served in infinite combinations, ranging from *Bolas de Berlim* to espressos. The strident voices of the night-shift factory workers began at 5:30 a.m., arriving with their rowdy motorbikes and arguing underneath our window about the futebol games yet to be played on the weekend.

You sit up in bed after the latest motorbike acceleration underneath our balcony window. Amari cries. Heather sleeps on.

"What kind of monster growls like that, Papá?" you say, panic trebling your dazed voice. You search for my hand.

I whisper a song from the Portuguese revolution about a seagull flying free to lullaby you and Amari back to sleep. I hope you doze for another hour before the woman in the apartment above starts her high-heeled pacing from room to room, making us believe she has slept with the stilettos on, considering her heels pounded until 2 a.m. Every day, the chair dragging is punctuated by fighting and swearing between this mother and her teenage son.

Clenched pen in hand, as would be expected of any writer practising nonviolent communication, I have written two notes verging on essays, verging on lectures about not wanting to be included in their lives of mutual verbal assault and door slamming, but such is life in crowded communities brought together by chance and porous brick walls.

Before the winter sun rises, we are awake, listening to the echo of high heels up and down the staircase bones which joins the loud

TVs, the barking dog three floors above. They travel the hollow
bones of our poorly built apartment, making me believe we live
inside a conch shell that traps every sound.

You sit up in bed rubbing your eyes, yawning, plunking your
body back down on the mattress after the latest door-banging.

"Why are those monsters burping and farting?"

I laugh. I hug you.

The perpetual noise is not truly noise; it is the continuous big
bang of creation, an everlasting reverberation, unstoppable, the
universe expanding neck and neck with the Portuguese national
debt. With it, I hope, my patience also expands. The incessant
honking, yelling, barking, and shouting are not yet understood
as pollution, considering the city itself begins its civic holiday celebrating its patron saint Anthony by releasing lengthy fireworks
at midnight, before a work and school day. Of course, the loud
festivity is read by a sleeping body as another middle-of-the-night
missile attack on the underground network of our nerves.

Again tonight, after you and Amari are asleep in bed, the roar of
a futebol goal from the pastry shop beneath, and in the woman
and son's apartment above, thunders through the building, jolting
you from your sleep.

"Is someone hurt?" you ask, clenching your eyelids in concern.

I lie next to you. Heather breastfeeds Amari. You clasp my
hand, snuggle closer. In time, your breath slows down, returns to
the peaceful lull of sleep.

I am not a believer in the sanctity of vaccines, yet I wait with
bated breath for the effectiveness of this noise inoculation in your
and Amari's psyches. By the time we return to Canada, we shall see
whether disruptive sounds provide lifelong immunity to auditory

pollution. If so, you are immunized to noise and will sleep like babies for the rest of your lives.

Bolo de Arroz e Sumo de Maracujá
(Rice Muffin and Passion fruit Juice)

150 g sugar	12 g baking powder
150 g wheat flour	3 eggs
75 g rice flour	Milk (up to 250 ml)
75 g butter	1 tsp vanilla extract
Lemon peel and sugar to please	

For three weeks, your kindergarten teacher, assistants, and a few parents have been measuring, cutting, and sewing the children's garments for the city's Carnival parade. The outfits will be a surprise for the parents, who have merely supplied black tights.

Carnival day arrives threatening rain, and along with other worried parents, I frown at the fast-moving clouds. Heather, Amari, and I drop you at the truck-long green gate and you are steered away deep into the town hall grounds where hundreds of children, adults, and seniors organize their parade groups. The voices swell; the crowds thicken.

I crane my neck, spot your kindergarten class assembled in a boy and girl pair pattern, making its way behind the first decorated float. The tractor pulls a trailer carrying a dozen reclining seniors disguised as clowns in cheerful kaleidoscope wigs, painted faces, and obligatory red noses. You are mesmerized. Your eyes have never encountered such a combination of wrinkles and blinding colours. Your grandmother Micas would never be caught in public wearing a fluorescent blue wig. I wave and smile. The cheerful seniors blow bubbles my way. I don't pop their colourful gifts.

You are among the first groups to exit the gates: forty children in red satin blouses, with white frilled cuffs and puffed shoulders, green berets hemmed in gold, sprinkling colour on the grey day. Despite your single layer of clothing and black tights, the cool, windy breeze does not draw a shiver from you. The first pair of children lead the long wake of your class, holding a cardboard caravel painted in white sails and red crosses. Your class celebrates Portugal's Age of Discoveries, and you are dressed up as a seventeenth-century navigator, Vasco da Gama or Diogo Cão, I surmise. You clear the gates into a sea of people for your first journey into performance. Unlike other children accustomed to their community's attention, you are serious and walk in a straight line. You see me, Heather, and Amari, forget your pose, give a shy wave.

This is your first exposure to Portuguese identity that is arrested in a backward gaze toward the self-perceived glory of the discoveries, an era of grandeur when the country set out on the tempestuous Atlantic as the Portuguese led Europe in pretending to discover lands already in existence. A voyage wrapped in the sails of a euphemism. In reality, the Portuguese led the way to conquer and annihilate, on a grand scale, a multitude of cultures around the globe. Those were the first steps toward the largest migration of people from Africa and Europe to the Americas, some by free will, most kidnapped for the lucrative slave trade.

My first Carnival, after arriving from Angola at your age, was less exuberant and colourful than this one. I dressed up in my eighty-year-old great-aunt Emilia's wool dress and frayed apron, folded in half and tied below my armpits. Even so, the garments dragged along the ground, lifting dust at my passage. In my hand was an old straw broom, taller than me, which offered meaning and anchor to my nervous hands. I strolled down your grandparents' lane and waited at the intersection, hoping to see and be seen. It was my first failed practice of ritualized social interactions. On my face, a plastic mask of an old woman hid me from embarrassment; unbeknownst to me, the households on my lane recognized who I was. Sitting on a stone, alone at the intersection, I soon grew bored. There was no parade in those times. I strolled back to the aged house, which matched my old drab garments. Since it was obligatory to have fun on such a day, I pretended that I enjoyed myself. I did not want to disappoint the world.

The worry lines on your olive-skin forehead deepen as you struggle to follow the more invisible language lines while singing along to Camões sonnets, attempting to follow a straight formation. Who can claim to count on thousands in the audience for their first public performance and in a second language? Your cousins Tomás and Simão, then Ti Filipe and Ti Marina wave. You return their greeting, smile, thankful for the anchor of recognition. They are proud to see you wearing your elaborate outfit while cradled by these hills, and before the eyes of a small city attempting to guess this blond boy's lineage. Several floats behind you, ten-year-olds with coal-smudged faces wear straw skirts and carry wooden spears and shields. In nobody's actions here do I detect an understanding of the racist or stereotypical assumptions that led to such a wardrobe choice. Your mother and I exchange glances and raise our eyebrows. Around us, the crowd applauds the charming and remarkable outfits of the little savages, who resemble the African cliché they believe in. The mind of the discoveries remains alive.

Francezinha e Fino (*Frenchie Sandwich and Beer on Tap*)

Sauce (Serves 2):

1 beer	1 glass of port wine
1 cube Knorr chicken stock	1 tbsp cornstarch
2 bay leaves	2 tbsp tomato paste
1 onion, chopped	1/2 cup milk
1 tbsp margarine	Piri-piri hot sauce to taste

Sandwich (Serves 1):

6 slices of bread piled high	4 frankfurters
2 slices of ham	2 smoked pork sausages
8 slices of cheese	1 steak

Serve topped off with a fried egg and French fries. This Portuguese baked sandwich, a speciality of Porto, is not for the fainthearted! To be eaten with a knife and fork.

Twice a month on a Saturday, I take our Tupperware container to the restaurant around the corner from your grandparents for our treat of fries. As you and I wait amid the cross-wafts of oil frying, chicken barbecuing, and salted cod boiling, an outsized rumbling burp draws our attention to four men lounging at a table, raising beer glasses and watching a futebol game on TV. Once your attention is captured, echoes of the first burp follow their spilled laughter. They wink at you. Repeat the soundtrack. Your eyes widen while your mouth stays open in soundless aftershock. You try to draw out a burp to match theirs. No luck.

The archeological relics from the four men's meals lie on the once-white linen. Since lunchtime, these men have been tongue-wrestling with cornbread and chicken kidneys swimming in a spicy onion tomato sauce. Cod fritter bits and black olive pits litter the floor. Vestiges of fries and mustard map the most recent tablecloth layer, beside pickled octopus and hints of the melted cheese of a fried Frenchie sandwich. Understandably, the men's exhausted bodies have collapsed against the backs of creaking chairs.

"Why are they so elephantic, Paulo?" you ask me, displaying awe and surprise—a question you might pose on seeing the size of an elephant for the first time.

"What do you think, Koah?"

You measure the scene as you watch one man struggling to press an excessively long sausage into his mouth.

"I guess they can't stop eating."

"And the only part of their bodies exercising is their eyes," I tell you, just as the man contradicts me and shakes his fist at the referee running on the screen, waving off a clamour for a penalty call.

Although pistol duels between honourable men have waned since past centuries, their psychic appeal lingers. This reinvented manly challenge can now be found in taverns or fancier Cambra restaurants, where the challengers replace bullets with sausage ammunition. Eating and drinking among men is an amicable duel at a table, an understated sport. The aim is to symbolically devour the challenger by out-eating and out-drinking him over the course of several hours, and through the courses of hors d'oeuvres, dispatching sausages and cheeses to eternity, aided by the flush of burgundy or beer. The metaphoric and emphatic battle is accomplished with the pride of athletes stretching their stomach and bowel muscles into round casks to accommodate the achievement. By the size of the bellies, this is a premier league match.

With a sigh, the larger man lifts his cap. His shirt sleeve wipes the sweat trapped in the folds of his nape. He shouts for another round. The champion grins and burps. He caresses his bulging belly, signalling there is still room to eat the opponents, were he not a gentleman. Only the pickled feet of chickens and pigs' ears remain uneaten on the plate, now marinating in cigarette smoke.

"Does he have a baby in his belly?" you ask, rubbing your own tummy, lifting your shirt for comparison.

The restaurant owner arrives breathless. He tussles your hair, before wrapping our fries in newspaper and folding them in a hat-like bundle. As usual, he dismisses my smallish container. The kitchen bell rings. He rushes away, only to appear at another door carrying a convoy of stewed tomato clam dishes toward the four men. Their glass-bottom beer salvo, clonking the table, greets the food. I was mistaken: the duel is yet to conclude. The men have been enjoying an interval before reloading the ammunition and pressing forth with the challenge: eye on the futebol match, tongues wrapped around steaming clam shells.

The expanded bellies' occasional bumping at the table causes the bottles crowded in the centre to exhale a collective crystalline moan. The glassy note resonates, suspended, stealing the attention from the futebol.

"It's not so hot today," you say, glancing outside the window at the rain washing away cigarette butts on the cobbled sidewalk. "Why are they so thirsty?"

The waiter, who is also the owner, the dishwasher, the cashier we are now waiting for in order to return our change, is also the bartender, the busboy, and likely the emergency second cook when his wife becomes overwhelmed at the stove. This juggler of trades offers to clear away the bottles from his customers' sight. In jest, the four men growl at his daring. By the decimation of empty wine and beer bottles at the table, the duel, which has been unfolding since lunchtime, will continue past dinner and into the night. The tall, fat, or skinny green or orange bottles stand like tombstones in an ever more crowded graveyard, displaying the dent inflicted on the liquor stock of the restaurant. At night's end, the bottles will be counted as if bodies on a battlefield. The winner will be decorated with the more golden hangover.

Pastel de Nata e Galão (Egg Tart and Latte)

Pastry:

600 g ready-made puff pastry	120 g sugar
6 egg yolks	300 ml cream
Cinnamon and powdered sugar to taste	

We return from a trip to the seaside fishing village of Furadouro, twenty kilometres away as the bird flies. However, we are not birds, and the gulls laugh at us from above.

"Why are we not moving, Paulo?"

"The light is red, Koah."

You are hungry and eager to arrive home. We are leaving the neighbouring town of Oliveira de Azeméis, about ten minutes from home. The light turns green. The car ahead does not move.

I squint, discern no one at the wheel. Behind me, cars honk in a domino sequence that resembles the penalty box soundtrack for *Hockey Night in Canada*. The approaching traffic on the other side moves steadily. "Why are we not moving, Paulo?"

"A car is blocking the road, Koah."

"Did they eat too much and die?"

I chuckle. "I hope not."

You stretch your neck, stiffen your legs, attempting to speed-grow another three centimetres for a better view from your car seat. You are worried. I am equally puzzled. I spot a man rushing out of a coffee shop, stepping onto the road, clinging to a pack of cigarettes, a newspaper, and a half-eaten *pastel de nata*. He waves apologetically before entering the idling car and speeding away just as the light turns red for us again.

I wonder how long the man had been stationed in the middle of the road before we arrived. I wonder if this is his daily pattern when returning from a work shift. I am not sure what to tell you. It is not uncommon in this region. Ayn Rand would be proud witnessing these virtues growing in this brave new town catching up to the world. Me, myself, and I, and no other in the civic equation.

We are nearly home and relieved. You sigh, recognizing the long Rua da Granja where we live. We follow one of the occasional tractors coming or going to the fields, chugging along the busy avenue, slowing down our urban zest for life in the fast lane. The only lane. A blend of two worlds lingers in the city, although even the slowing down is a partial speeding up. In my time, the slowing down was accomplished at the wheels of ox-pulled wagons filled with manure, clogging the thinner car traffic.

The tractor veers left, and we speed up past the butcher shop, the photo studio, the spa. When I am about to turn off to our driveway and parking spot behind the building, we encounter a parked car blocking access. I sigh. Honk. This happens several times an hour throughout the day. Since I cannot turn, the traffic behind me also cannot carry on. Several cars honk. We wait until we continue to wait a little more. It is now an eternity. The car radio news announces a costly increase to Portuguese bonds after another financial study confirmed the inefficiency of the Portuguese economy on the world stage. Welcome to the land of forced slowness.

You complain of hunger. The drifting aroma of pastries from the bakery adds to your torture. A woman leaves the shop, balancing two innocent boxes of pastries on one hand and talking on her cellphone. She enters her vehicle, sits a little longer in the car to finish the phone conversation. Eventually the woman drives away amid the honking cars, without a gesture of atonement for her mischief. Ten metres further along the street, two other parking spaces sit empty, inconveniently away from the bakery entrance.

We veer into the driveway, park the car, and walk to the bakery on the way to our apartment. We line up to buy freshly baked *pão da avó* buns to stave off your hunger.

On the TV above the counter, a documentary about the new Pope Francis draws your attention.

"Who is that?" You point to the man in absolute white.

"The pope, Koah."

"What is that?"

A fine question. It sets me up for a challenge, explaining in the wink of a fifteen-second TV commercial what religion and Christianity represent. The images move to a picture of a pastry-white robed Pope Francis kneeling in contrition at a confessional, and so moves your attention span.

"What's he doing?"

You are following the images with more attention than you would follow a cartoon on the screen.

"He is telling another priest the things he regrets and which he hopes next time to do differently."

"Like what?" you ask.

"Like when his words hurt other people, or the times he was not thoughtful about others. Do you think that is a good idea?"

Your solemn nod tells me you think that is an important moment in every life and worthy of any belief system.

The bakery owner fills the paper bag with four large buns, tries out his English on you from his emigration years in Australia. Then he turns to me and complains about bureaucracy, the lack of civility in day-to-day life, lowering his voice to a whisper to confide his regret in having returned to Portugal. Before waving us off, he offers you a Kinder chocolate egg that you accept with delight. I place my arm over your shoulder. You lean into me as we walk outside and upstairs to our apartment to end our day of adventure on the Atlantic coast. We will eat your favourite rotini for dinner, before falling asleep in our Cambra valley.

the land
of the leaving

Para venir a lo que no eres
  (To become what you are not)
Has de ir por donde no eres
  (You must travel to where you are not)
—SOR JUANA INÉS DE LA CRUZ

How long will you stay in Portugal? This is the question grandparents collecting grandchildren in your schoolyard ask. They want
to know if we would be tempted to settle, especially you, Koah.
"He must love it here," they say, half guessing, half hoping to tip
the scale of country affections in their favour. "His grandparents
would be so happy," they assure us. "To be severed from the wee

ones is our hardest life cross." Their voices lowered to a whisper. A poorly kept secret.

· These elders know better than most how distance tears a heart. Portugal is a land of emigrants. Perhaps more than half the people have left this valley, and the surrounding hills, to seek a better life in Ontario, Venezuela, Newark, South Africa, Paris, and Germany, most in the 1960s; others earlier in the twentieth century, to Brazil. In this decade, fifty years later, a renewed wave of departures has crested. Your own kindergarten teacher Skypes nightly with her twenty-something engineer son in the United Kingdom. These recent emigrants are no longer cleaners, construction labourers, domestic helpers, and factory workers. The present exodus includes nurses and teachers, computer and trades people, university graduates. Unlike the previous emigration wave, this is a brain drain of highly skilled workers. The national repercussions will be vaster and longer lasting, bringing continued impoverishment to the public coffers. In addition to three years of free daycare, Portugal schooled and trained its future professionals for sixteen years of nearly free education, only for other nations to harvest the benefits of such citizen investment.

On your grandparents' lane, six of the children who shared my childhood of hopscotch, futebol, skipping rope, and hide-and-seek have left the country, never to return. Australia and Switzerland, France, Brussels, and Canada offered them a ladder of hope. Their grandchildren will not speak their mother tongue. There is hardly a family in 147 square kilometres of Vale de Cambra that does not have one who left their summer closet collecting dust and their toys rusting in nostalgia.

At your school gate, a man, picking up his grandchild, stops me. He says, "Do you recognize me?"

It takes me a second to erase the wrinkles and to paint over the white hairs not in my memory. "I do."

He is the father of a childhood friend with whom I played futebol on the roads, patios, and in the woods. His family of five lived in a garage on my street. Lowering his eyes, he confided with a sigh that he had not seen his son in nine years. Before that visit, he had not seen Carlitos in another nine years. He has seen his now teenaged granddaughters only twice in their lives. This forced clan separation, caused by economic imperatives, brings a festering grief to a culture whose extended family ties are the foundation of community existence. This is the silence they must leave behind to find a daily meal.

Technological tricks pretend to erase the distance by placing images and voices at our fingertips, yet those visions on a screen will never warm the body with their embrace. Ironically, your aunt Marina and grandmother Micas, living two hundred metres apart, interact through cellphones more often than face to face. Near and far, families have departed into screens and computer chips. It is a newly invented static emigration facilitated by technology. The machines are a band-aid that patch but do not fill the gap growing larger inside the heart.

My physical emigration makes emptiness more visible and obvious, and therefore a blessing: our sadness and distance cannot be fooled by a screen any more than fast-food fries and pop can satiate our hunger and thirst. Your computer-illiterate grandparents cannot see you on a weekly Skype call that brings movement and voice that much closer for a more thorough fooling of the senses, yet not the wiser spirit. So your cascading laugh and sparkling eyes will disappear for your grandparents after our return to Canada. The photos by their bedside will remain imprints to aid their memory but are insufficient to replace you, and this is as it should be. The heart and the spirit see through the fog of screens.

I did not need to leave this valley for economic imperatives. I am a cultural refugee from undernourishment and stagnation, born to a community whose priorities include free meals at election times, a vanity church tower, and a misplaced memorial gymnasium project to stick a name to, but no money to fix your leaky kindergarten roof or sufficient funds to staff schools. Therefore two neighbourhood schools, as well as yours, are slated to close next year.

From the time I remember seeking a sense of personal identity, the raft of books by my bedside offered me an escape to wider horizons where the sensitive, kinder, more thoughtful worlds of my imagination found closer affinities. I departed in my mind first, sailing with Marco Polo on his Silk Route travels; I sat in a Paris café, eavesdropping on the conversations of de Beauvoir and Sartre, while the Catholic-induced fog in my mind dissipated for the rest of eternity. Day by day, book by book, my dreams strengthened my resolve, and I began to trust that my leap of faith would not land me in another existential void. I believed in my intuition, my vision, my abilities. Hitchhiking out, I stood at the edge of town on the cobblestone road, my thumb pointing away from the hills.

You and I walk back from school along the descending labyrinthine lanes to the irrigation channel for our daily boat race, passing many houses with sealed window shutters. The sunshine only enters these rooms when the emigrants arrive for their summer visits or for the rare Christmas appearance.

The emigrant who can afford to visit the valley does not stay long enough to become irritated at the old ways of doing and being. Our five-month stay has drawn the curiosity of those who ask if I have returned to settle back home with my Canadian family. Their eyes reveal a blend of puzzlement and hope. Did the pull of extended family roots win over an economic imperative? Were they right in having stayed? Is it true that there is nothing better than the place where we were raised, despite the history of poverty, exploitation, oppression, and a social failing to catch up to the times of more open-mindedness and new opportunities?

"Why is that roof so huge?" you ask, pointing at an enormous house designed with a steep drooping roof that resembles the oversized wings of a crouching bird.

The changes emigrants bring in their swift visits leave indelible footprints in the landscape, yet little lasting roots in the minds of Cambra residents. The mark is seen in the steep roofs of their summer homes, mimicking those in the Swiss and French Alps, yet out of place in a valley where snow does not fall. The grandiose house designs signal financial success, an imposing presence to compensate for the emigrant's absence, a perpetual howl to make up for their reluctant disappearance from the community of their birth.

I and others who left in youth will soon be forgotten, our faces no longer recognized after decades of absence. I am no longer familiar with the new generations, and my anonymity will only grow, since most of my childhood generation is now scattered around the country and the globe.

Although I have settled far away, I never doubted the depth of my roots, the harbour of our Matos's two-hundred-year-old walls. Every cell in my body understood that this roof would always be here to shelter me, regardless of how far my dreams would take me. In truth, it was the strength of our roots that allowed the long reach of my flight. I understood that I could soar high, as a kite unrolling my never-ending tail, for I trusted the steady hand of family would never let me go and that I would never be lost. I had the privilege of following the wind and my whims, knowing any fall would reel me home into the open arms of extended family. I hope that you, Koah, and Amari will also grow up feeling and seeing those roots, and that you will never be lost.

You do not appear to notice the absence of children along our home-from-school route past deserted patios, or the quiet lanes sprinkled with the occasional elder sunning in a doorway.

As you and I approach your grandparents' gate, we are halted by a neighbour in his fifties, who lived in Montreal and who unwillingly returned to assist in his wife's health recovery and be near his school-aged daughter. Having experienced another world, he now feels even more trapped than before. "I'm paid a little over minimum wage to be a draughtsman. I see hunger all around me." It is no longer the speculative mirage of an improved life; he has a measure of comparison. A memory of a better life. "In Canada, I earned enough to live comfortably."

Of the twins in your class, whose mother was born in Montreal and arrived in the valley at the age of eight, their grand-mother confided, "We wanted to return to Portugal before my children grew old enough not to want to leave Canada," she says, a smile of relief on her face. The strategy proved wise. Few teenagers wish to settle into a new place, leaving behind their personal history and their day-to-day loves. The quaint Cambra valley memories belong to the parent emigrant; they are nothing but a quirky holiday movie for their visiting children, not the road to their future.

In your first month of kindergarten, the teachers took you to visit the museum, then to the library for puppet storytime, and had you splashing in the indoor pool. On weekends, you watch your cousins' roller hockey games, and then walk into the wooden rink to kick the heavy ball, simply to experience their sports territory. In my childhood, I kicked a football between two stones for a goal. Your grandfather Agosto played barefoot so as not to damage his one pair of shoes. In his only family portrait, he is six years old and wears dress shoes borrowed from the photographer's studio. I had to move to a city to finish high school and only then set foot in a gymnasium. There was no swimming pool in this valley. Now, a mobile library van arrives weekly at your school to bring books to those children whose parents do not think of taking them near books. This may explain the town's modern library often having more staff than patrons, with many books collecting dust. Sometimes the books I borrow require cataloguing in the computer-based tag system for their first journey into the sun.

The Cambra valley has moved in time at the pace of the garden snail climbing up the collard stalks that grow as tall as me and resemble small trees. In this land of rain, the collards climb faster than the snail lagging behind. The tender leaves are never reached. I do not know whether my impetus to keep moving to the edges of new thought and exploration makes my vision of an open-minded, thriving, creative community here just as far-fetched as when I thumbed away. The occasional wind of change sweeping through other parts of Portugal misses this valley tucked in its comforts and conveniences. It is no wonder that even those born here and choosing to continue speaking their mother tongue still migrate to Lisbon or Porto, where the cross-sweep of ideas is more likely to occur.

After talking with the neighbour, we arrive at the portico to your grandparents' kitchen. The fishmonger, stooped over from the weight of her seven decades and from the wooden crate on her head, insists that your grandmother Micas needs a sole for dinner. Dark blood drips from the limp fish in her hand onto the clean entrance tile. This draws more attention from your grandmother than the aggressive pitch from the woman, who is not taking no for an answer. It is a type of word fencing. The fishmonger hopes your grandmother will acquiesce just to stop the pestering. For the arthritic elder, a sale is a sale, another day of work when her failure might mean begging on the street, since she is the last monger, on foot, hawking her fish in the weave of these lanes. Your grandmother Micas buys the sole, plus two large mackerel.

For all its faults and unsung glories, the Cambra community is a rarity. Despite its ruts and stagnations, the rovers and the seekers, like me, do return to find harbour. The surrounding hills offer a steadfast retreat, a buffer from the anxious crossroads and stormy winds of choice.

I bow to the self-sacrificing family and neighbours, who tend and attend to their birth community. I bow to school friends who accepted their curtailed dreams behind the slow progress of a centipede tripping over its forty-four-thousand legs. Year after year, the people who welcome or roll their eyes at me are a joy to recognize, if only for their role in the irritating script of small-town drama. Here everyone lives inextricably connected, and the script repeats itself with the cycle of the seasons. There is a sigh of comfort in arriving at a land that recognizes me despite the passage of time etching its tracks on my skin. To the town, I also nod in recognition for its growing asphalt and cement scars crowding its surface.

"Are you back to visit our shithole of a country?"

"Corrupt politicians run our lives."

"Nothing works smoothly in this land."

The prayer wheel of complaining from family and friends becomes a love prayer, a tribute to what they believe cannot be changed and what they cannot live without. It requires rare resilience and stillness of mind to remain where one was born. To live in this valley is to accept what is, a lay spiritual path of continuous surrender. It is to live through hair-pulling frustrations or deep delights and remain unmoved, tolerating the ground they sprang from, which later, or sooner, will collect them again into its fold.

At four years old, you have already journeyed many times between Europe and North America. From this land of the leaving, you have inherited the propensity to move about the planet at a frequency your ancestors never imagined possible, a frequency that leaves an ecological footprint larger than centuries of our ancestors' lives combined. In order to visit her daughter, your great-grandmother Clotilde once went to Lisbon, three hundred kilometres away. That is also as far as your great-grandfather Manuel da Costa ever travelled. I, on the other hand, have lived in several countries over four continents and crossed dozens and dozens of borders. Days before your great-grandfather Manuel da Costa died, he received my postcard from China, five months into my two-year journey circum-backpacking the world. He showed the postcard proudly to his friends at the market or in the village hub. The day he died, my postcard was still tucked in his shirt pocket.

I wonder how many places you will leave in your life, and what will prompt you to say farewell. I wonder where you will feel at home and find your community of choice, versus a community of chance, whether your options will be vast or shrink under the political winds of protectionism. Will you move over mountains and cross hemispheres for love, as I did? I wonder if climate change, pandemics, environmental disasters, or new wars will force you to move from your home against your will. I remember my heartache in leaving Luanda at your age, the warm ocean landscape receding from the plane window, the ache of leaving my beloved red chair behind, a migration against my desire. A force larger than my will had reshaped my universe.

You are only four years old and have already experienced a sense of two homes, a migratory bird at ease in two continents and landscapes. You carry in you the desire for movement and the joy of discovering the new. *Adventure* is already your favourite word.

It is too early to anticipate what role this Cambra valley and these people will bestow on your future or your heart. What has been learned from emigration history suggests that your years of visiting Portugal will simply become a repository of our family memory until the day you establish your own family. The Cambra valley will then recede into the background of your experiences and identity. A dormant seed? Or a brief chapter of our family history to be remembered?

the birthing stones

The rain-fed torrent leaps off the granite lip of the Serra da Freita escarpment where, concealed by the dense vegetation in the gully bottom, the waterfall drops into the three terraced pools I swam in during my youth.

"The highest cascade in the Iberian Peninsula." The claim to tallest fame does not etch an impression on your four-year-old mind.

Little by fast, dark by wide, arriving from the mountain range across, a spill of clouds stains the horizon until it smears the faraway thread of the Mizarela waterfall on its seventy-five-metre dive.

"Here is the snow I promised you, Koah."

"Brrrr," you say as you shake. Unannounced, the weather is dropping in on us. I help you zip up your wind jacket as the first flakes of cold land on your nose. You screech and jump in delight.

The snow arrives, albeit two months late and not for Christmas, when it was in every child's imagination. You are not complaining. Any geography, any season is time for snow in your limitless universe.

"How come this white stuff colours my hands red?" You gather handfuls, surprised at the immediate red imprint it makes on the skin. Your hands mould a frosty ball and hurl it at me. It is ironic that you, a Canadian boy, had to travel to the Portuguese highlands to experience your first snowball toss.

We rush for shelter in Castanheira, the nearby village, across from the quarry of biotite nodules—a rare geological occurrence of scaly golden stones embedded in granite, which the locals named birthing stones, for they pop out of their mother stones. Last year, an interpretive centre officialized the site as a tourist attraction.

We walk down the steep cobbled lane, careful not to slip on the wet stones polished by centuries of passing hooves and feet, now waxed by the sleet. The village's black slate roofs glisten. The vicious wind that finds us will also find the gaps in stone walls and bite the villagers huddled around fireplaces inside.

The ding-a-long, gong-a-song of brass bells, crisp and resonant, reverberates off the stone. We stop at the fork in the lane, then tilt our heads, tuning our ears two octaves above the whistling wind. The cattle sound their return from a day of roaming freely in the meadows and will find their corrals on the ground level of every house. They sensed the premature disappearance of daylight and the advancing storm. We press our backs against a wall, not knowing from where the cattle will appear.

The castanets of hooves on stone signal their proximity. From such a narrow lane, where I imagine widowers could lean rosy cheeks across bedroom windows and kiss, a bull twice your height stops. He stares, surprised at the visitors in his path. After a brief snort, he essays a few steps toward us. "Ohhh…" you say, as your eyes widen and your body nudges closer to mine. Even I hold my breath, admiring the long twisting horns ending in a sharp duo of deadly spears. The eyes well above your height meet your gaze. "They are ginormous," you say, unusually slowly, revealing reverence in your voice. I guide us to the exterior stone stairway of a crumbling house. We climb three steps. The orange on the bull's fur glistens, polished by the falling snowflakes. Their presence brightens the uniform grey of the surrounding granite that frames the street. The luxuriant black of the slate roofs no longer steals our eyes' attention.

The bull snorts, then moves its chiming song along, followed by six more cattle. One by one, they disappear inside separate corrals the way a human would on the return home after a day of earning their daily bread. Soon after, someone in each house ambles down from their living quarters above the corral to drop the crossbar across the heavy wooden door, sealing the animals in for the night, a custom from a time when these hills could still hear the wolf's howl under the full moon.

I tap your shoulder again. You are staring down the lane where the cattle have disappeared into each house as if the promenade of bulls had not stopped, as if the bells had not silenced. The snowflakes pile on the brim of your hood. I flick a snowflake on your face. Startled, you laugh, grab a handful from the step above us, and find my bull's eye. I place my splayed hands upright on my head and roar, "Run for your life."

We run with the wind behind us to a meadow by the road that displays a brown historical marker. You are not interested in hearing me read the legends on the interpretive signs. Instead we play tag, leaping back and forth over the low wall of a dolmen, our feet finding the occasional puddle hidden among the heather. The snow is too wet to stay on the ground.

"What's this mess of stones doing here?" you ask between laughs, attempting to catch your breath in the crosswind that slaps our faces and robs our air. The fierce wind requires me to shout. We lean toward the invisible force, walk onward.

"These are the remnants of structures from people who lived here long, long ago."

These hills have been a crossroads of many waves of peaceful and forceful occupations. We find cultural tracks such as the Bronze Age tumulus and the cromlech walls that we are hopping over in a game of tag. These meadows still hide traces of Celtic, Roman, and Arabic passage. Soon we will walk the quaint stone bridge on the Roman road built in the second century CE.

In the first century BCE, the Celts would have felt at home when they reached the crest of Serra da Freita, climbing a thousand metres into the sky, and were offered a glimmer of the sea. The granite-quilted land, the gorse-infused air echoed another highland left behind on the British Isles. Your genetic roots link the Celtic people who inhabited these promontories in the second century CE with your Scottish highland roots on your maternal grandfather Robert's side. Across the Atlantic, a thousand miles' ride on the back of a raven, your far-off Celtic ancestry intersects in these highlands. In landscape and in flesh, your ancient past meets you here for the first time.

In a few short years, hauling backpacks on our backs, I will bring you to Serra da Freita again for an extended pilgrimage through the ages to find *citânias* (Celtic fortified villages), menhirs, and Neolithic rock art scattered through the meadows and gullies. Together, our fingers will trace the circles, spirals, triangles, and other symbols etched on those boulders. I'll explain that two thousand years ago this Gralheira massif sheltered a runaway branch of your distant Scottish past, and that they have waited for you to arrive and meet your Portuguese present. These stones mark the place where the DNA of your past has met the DNA of your present through your mother and me. In a cosmic trail of human migrations, the separated tribes have entwined again twenty-two centuries later. So today, on the hills of northern Portugal, one encounters blond and light-eyed people like you.

Your stone age began on the day you left the cradle to crawl in rapture over the pebbled beach of Clover Point in Victoria. Perhaps in the genes, perhaps in close proximity to the land, the texture, shape, and colour of rocks at once enthralled you. From that first day, you became invested in living closer to stones—and since your mother and I are no longer nomads among rugged landscapes—you bring your treasures home to hide under your pillow or your placemat. In the dryer's tumbler, we find striking black basalt or green agates, yellow-green epidotes or rust-red jasper, a variety of rock shapes living in your pants or shirt pockets. Our foyer sees a mineral pile grow by the shoe rack after each park outing. Inside tiny pockets, you have smuggled granite and greywacke across airport security. The guards shrug and smile after evaluating the danger of a small stone weapon in your hands on a long-haul flight.

"It's freezing, Koah. Let's hop in the car." I bend low to fool a knock-down wind.

As usual, you are crouched over the ground; your fingers dig. You stand up and wave. You have found the quartz abundant in this mountain range. A tiny one. Sometimes I notice those angelic shells by their returning glimmer in the sun, watching me. Both your Portuguese great-grandfathers collected quartz from this terrain. I remember the pumpkin-sized quartz embedded with purple crystals. They lined the corn-threshing patio, and my hands could not lift them. Your gaze, while holding up your prize among this sea of rock, may indeed have ancestor resonance, as megalithic and Celtic peoples venerated their stone.

The dance between hand and stone survives today in this country of skillful stonemasons reshaping the hardened earth into contemporary visions of beauty. You see it every day in the blue basalt designs against limestone-cobbled sidewalks where you enjoy skipping and hopping along patterned anchors and stars, flowers and mermaids.

One day, I will tell you that your paternal grandmother's side of the family, now settled on the Cambra valley bottom for five generations, also walked down from these hills in the 1800s, hailing from the village of Rocas do Vouga. My childhood blond hair might be a genetic echo of that lineage map. Perhaps mountains and rock are embedded in our bones, and that is why when my eyes lighted on the Canadian Rocky Mountains for the first time, my feet turned into stone, and I stayed in Alberta. I married that first time in the wilds of Banff National Park by the Bow River; the justice of the peace, huffing and puffing, climbed the Hoodoos Trail, stopping often, pleading to know if the marrying spot was far. After the vows, the clothes slid off and I dove into the glacier-fed waters for the true shivering and blessing. I settled in the Rockies, or its foothills, for years, and like your great-grandfather Matos in his Freita stomping grounds, I disappeared into the mountainous silence in the company of my thoughts. Those weekly incursions into the towering cathedrals of dolomite populated by bears, porcupine, and elk were a treasure hunt to find the hidden parts of my spirit buried beneath the human culture that had insisted I suit and tie my body, lip-stick my mind.

My exposed hands quickly rust out in this Freita snowstorm. The fingers move in slow motion. They find the car door handle. I call you again. You arrive running, the quartz prize clutched high above your head. The blizzard lands upon us full force, and I drive with caution along the twisting, slippery road toward the valley bottom. We make slow progress by one of the many passes on this mountain range, marvel at a granite church signalling the latest sequence of people to leave a marker of their beliefs on this landscape. In a thousand years, our descendants will also admire the seven enormous crosses chiselled from granite marking the walking route to the church and recreating the Calvary.

This sea-bound land that defines Portugal became a meeting place at the beginning of what is now called Europe. At this crossroads of sailors, our Phoenician, Greek, Roman, Celtic, Carthaginian, Swabian, Arabic, and African blood flows through the veins of nearly every body walking these political boundaries; even before the navigators sailed away in the fifteenth century to further mix the genetic pot of the planet. In 700 BCE when the Celts arrived, the Gralheira massif belonged to a county called Portucale. This land and this people are a hymn to cross-pollination and the genetic impetus for receiving and expanding into newness, despite the blood atrocities of history committed in the process. All these people, all this past history is also you, my son. This vast heritage of peoples is your strength, sorrow, and beauty, a tapestry that is not woven of one thread only. These true roots expose any false claims of racial or ethnic purity, here or anywhere.

You eat your picnic of bread and cheese, yogurt and orange in the backseat of your grandfather's car, marvelling at the whiteout that envelops us. Halfway down, the storm vanishes into another dream. The green terraced fields return without a hint of the icy winds and the blistering snow curtains that settled at the top.

Two days later, we return to Serra da Freita. There are no traces of the snowstorm that touched the landscape. It is another day and another dream of living. The sun, wind, and heather, the stones and earth drank the moisture. We sit between tall boulders on the edge of the river Caima, which in a hundred metres will become the Mizarela waterfall. After tossing pebbles into the rapidly moving water and cheering the loud plonks, you climb these boulders that lift you higher than your fears. You enjoy the wider view to the wind turbines on the distant ridges. Then you spread your arms, and your blue jacket billows. A curious swallow swoops near your head.

"The swallow mistook you for a juicy mosquito." I wink.

After you tire of scrambling up and down the boulders that make you slip and cling to conquer their top, you settle below me, digging the ground again.

"Did you know your great-grandfather Matos walked these hills every autumn tracking wild animals?"

"What for?"

"To hunt them."

"That is not very nice." You look up from your digging, your nose shrivelling up.

Most of his life, your great-grandfather Matos retreated to the Freita hills to be alone with his hunting dog, Chancas (*clog shoe*), and to be true to the meaning of his family name, *woods*. After a steep day's climb from the valley bottom, he tramped about for days. Once among the heights, he would criss-cross the gullies and escarpments hunting for partridge, fox, wolf, hare. This is how some men demonstrated their love of solitude and of the outdoors. By harming it.

Throughout my childhood, I cringed at the splayed fox pelts with hollowed sockets, toothless agape mouths spread on the dining room floorboards, which your great-grandfather encouraged me to pet and admire. I always avoided those macabre rugs and tiptoed past that chilling corner of the house.

Hunting evolved as a socially accepted justification for your great-grandfather Matos and preceding generations to disappear and commune with the earth, and it was sport to many others, too, who enjoyed the adrenaline rush from killing. His son, your great-uncle José Maria, followed his hunting footsteps on these Freita hills, and he expanded his firing range further afield into the southern plains and the northern border forests of the nation. He has already introduced you to the embalmed birds, badgers, and other creatures in his hallway glass display. He is proud to point to the royal eagle shot near the Salamanca provincial border as it glided out of its protected Spanish nature park. In Portugal, this eagle species had vanished for some time, and now it is nearly extinct in the Iberian Peninsula. The family hunting tradition has died out now that your great-uncle José Maria is in his eighties and too weak to climb the rugged terrain with shotgun in hand. The family hunting mind survives in the video games your cousins play where the stakes have evolved to hunting humans and monsters in fast-moving bytes.

Ultimately, our family has left the animals in peace at Serra da Freita. Although by arriving at this mountain plateau in a gasoline-powered vehicle and not on foot, we, too, have caused far-reaching harm to nature, to creatures near and far, to other peoples and lands elsewhere on the planet. Nevertheless, you and I invent less harmful games in the woods today. Or no games at all. We sit in and with the quiet, learning from the stillness and the courageous winged or lizard visitors that arrive full of curiosity to teach us belonging and coexistence. The quad- and motorcycle-chewed trails on surrounding landscape paths demonstrate that the hills are still held ransom by the mind that seeks the away, yet brings along its restless longings and poisonous machines to pollute the silence. It is with the unstill mind that pollution begins.

"Come to eat our picnic and enjoy this magnificent view."

In the distance, the cinder-bone mountain ranges hem in the horizon beyond the Caima waters gurgling below us. Gigantic white windmill blades churn the westerlies in the heights and help make Portugal's electrical power grid run fully on renewable energies.

You continue digging and sliding these mineral discoveries into your jacket pockets, now bulging with the rocks that you must bring home. "They are special," you assure me, climbing up the boulder to join me. The black-freckled granite, the fish-shaped basalt in your hands, you bring closer to my eye. Your delighted grin in sharing your treasures meets my delighted grin in sharing your delight. Each quartz or granite holds a story, carries a meaning you alone have attributed to it. One day you will recognize you love a stone like you love a dear friend. In their holding of silence, they amplify the little voice inside you, the solid foundation of your being that needs surrounding quiet to be heard, to be listened to the way mountains know how. Stones teach you the practice of listening to the interior landscape that you can map best. The rest of the world, from school to church, will make you listen to the outside, force your own voice silent so as to be talked to, to follow, and to be moulded.

Another day ends on the crest of Serra da Freita. The breeze arrives to tickle the clouds to bed, to push the sun toward the sea and out of sight behind us. There it will sleep among beds of sea-weed. While we finish our cornbread and sheep's cheese, the birds linger, awaiting our inadvertent gifts. We have let the landscape see us, and our peaceful intentions become part of it. We have gone inside ourselves to find our place in the universe, and we have returned. You have also returned holding one more quartz in your hand, so that your stone-filled pockets will anchor your memories to these hills.

Reluctantly, we rise to our feet atop the boulder in this land once trodden by an ancient tribe we call the Lusitanian people. Few today follow the maze of trails to our ancestral tribe of Celtic origin. These hills are our sanctuary.

We shall return.

We shall return often.

learning to shave,
learning to leave

In the third week of March, we walk home from your school among fields sprouting onion, carrot, and fava crops, smelling this fragrant equinox green in the air. You hum your excitement at the thought of keeping a surprise from me after your class prepared a Father's Day event for tomorrow, the first day of the two-week Easter break. The days now stretch the light farther across the sky, reach more blooming flowers and more nests of *melros* already chirping. Every few steps, a song line you are learning in perfect Portuguese slips from your lips. Covering your mouth, you glance at me.

"Nada. Não foi nada."

I pretend I am distracted spotting a nest in the oak grove.

You speak to me in Portuguese as if this language had never been separated from your heart. My own hums upon hearing Portuguese words pouring from your mouth. It is the sound of an ancient stream, now reawakened on its own soil, a thinning vein that almost dried in you, despite my daily efforts in Canada. This is the resuscitation of anything once given up for dead. This is the genuine miracle. Help yourself and God will help you too. Months later, back in Victoria, people will smile when you speak in English; you speak it with my Portuguese accent, the *i* long and lilting.

The long-awaited Saturday arrives and you rise before the sun. Every few minutes, between spoonfuls of porridge, you ask if it is time. Your tummy hurts, and I imagine performance anxiety already fills you with the metaphorical butterflies of anticipation. You leave your porridge uneaten and do not even pick out the blueberries, your favourite. It is understandable: a stomach full of butterflies has no room for berries.

Next to your friends, pressed in the three rows of long benches, you wave, as every father cranes his neck, also pressing one another for a better photo angle. You are growing pale and can hardly accompany your schoolmates in the songs eagerly memorized that week. The paleness in your face and the glassy eyes show me you are struggling. You manage to hold it together, and by the end of the performance, you are not voicing any of the words.

I do not wait for the applause to finish and go meet you on the bench.

"Papá, I feel sick."

You cannot stand. I rush you in my arms to the bathroom, weaving between the pressed bodies, and we nearly reach it in time, before the yellow and green vomit sprays me, the toilet lid, and the surrounding white tile floor.

Tonight a high fever laps around in your veins. In a faint voice, you ask for water, eyes struggling to let the light in. You reach for my hand, wanting to feel my hold on you as I place a cold damp cloth on your forehead. I squeeze your shoulder for reassurance. You mumble the first song lines you had proudly memorized in Portuguese and which now breathe at the surface of your being.

Pai, és tão alto como o céu... (Father, you are as tall as the sky...)

You tell me you do not wish to die today. I assure you that it is not about to happen.

"Why do you wonder about dying?"

You fall silent.

I attempt to read the answer in your eyes. You look away. I lie next to you on the sofa with the fairy-tale storybook on my chest, listening to your laboured breathing, the radiant fever of your body overheating mine.

My wandering gaze finds fallen lint balls under the desk, discovers new chips in the tile flooring, the brittle skeletons of crumbs in the gaps between the indigo cushions. My gaze at last assembles the scattered thoughts that have spun without root in the whirlwind of the day. I release an *aha*.

"I think I understand what is in your mind, Koah."

Even before you started to walk, you were shown the picture of your mother's deceased parents holding her as a six-month-old baby. When you said you wanted to see Grandma Joyce to give her a hug, we explained the dead cannot be hugged. "Why did she die?" Your mother and I explained that Joyce had been ill for a long, long time and never recovered.

Today you have vomited and feel the weight of a fever. Today you taste the failing of your invincible four-year-old body. The proximity of illness brings you the fear that this is the first taste of death, imagining it around the corner, ready to take you away as it did your mother's parents. One day I will explain to you that cancer also took away Maria Teresa, my grandmother, and your great-aunt Maria whom you never met.

After we tell each other the things we appreciated best about this day—of which few will rest in memory—and after the bed-time stories, you weave hands and legs with mine, entangling me in a knot that ensures I will not leave as you slip into sleep. From your infant days, you resist falling into the night. I imagine you experience slumber as a type of death to your mind, the light vanishing as your eyes close, the eyelids teetering on the edge of consciousness and you about to disappear. It is a type of departure from those you love, and so you hold onto my hand until your fingers uncurl, your legs twitch, and you drop into the dream world.

I do not remember cuddling with my father or sleeping on the same bed. My father does say that as a toddler, I would spread out in their bed and push him and my mother off, attempting to stay cool during the hot African nights of Luanda. From his memory, I learn that not all my experiences are stored in memory, and that contrary to my assumption, we did share the same bed.

Fatherhood provides an opportunity to make my world anew, fostering hope buoyed by your boundless energy. For those of us cherishing the last memories of blue whales in the oceans and garbage-free rivers, it is our chance to reinvent the future together. I remember my tender ages and what hurt or elated me. I remember the joy of having my father present on weekends. On weekdays, he disappeared before I woke up, returning at 8 p.m. after an hour-long commute, wearing a smile of exhaustion and revealing little energy to match my excitement. Only now do I understand this was a father who preferred to travel long days and return home every day than remain at the airbase until the weekend. He would rather see me and my sister in our sleep, even if only for a few minutes daily, than not at all. This is the same father who shortened his military career in his forties to be home with his family. But soon after that, I left for university.

The joyous memory of riding my father's shoulders in a maze throughout the entire house as if he were an airplane lost from his airbase remains etched in my heart as a rare moment of play before bed. A moment that even in my exhaustion I will give you, Koah, so you can fall asleep, brightening your night dreams with a smile.

This is also my time to remake fatherhood and stand up to the economic forces that expect me to give most of my life to a job rather than to my family, friends, and community. So I stay home in your early years and write in the cracks of time with the orchard owls hooting for company.

The day following the Father's Day performance, Doctor Jorge confirmed my suspicion of chickenpox as the blisters soon spread at comet speed across your face and torso. You caught it from a classmate, and soon others develop it during their Easter break. Two weeks later, your sister Amari will follow.

For those two weeks, we stay indoors longer than usual and play Lego, draw, watch *Noddy* videos for a special treat.

This afternoon, after reading you a book and while you lie on the couch, I walk to my pile of loose papers on the desk at the corner.

"I'm going to do a little writing."

"Don't go, Paulo. Why do you have to go?"

"To do my work, Koah."

"Why do you need to work?"

"You love reading books. I write books."

"Paulo, you don't need to write more books. We have so many already."

You point to the shelves overflowing with books in different sizes, thicknesses, and languages.

"The library has even more books, you know?"

You nod with the certainty of the obvious, the confidence of a foolproof argument.

"Perhaps this could be my last book," I say, waving the sheets filled with scribbles. "I'd like to write more stories for a book I am really enjoying writing. And you might even like reading it one day. Who knows?"

I leave it at that mystery and leave you to play Lego on the sofa, three steps away from me.

After a few minutes, showing a serious face, the face of one who has been pondering the question, you stop your play and tell me, "We should write a book together one day."

I raise my eyebrows in surprise and delight. "I'd like that very much."

"Good. We'll do that then," you say, returning your attention to the Lego speedboat you are assembling.

I contemplate spoiling my future surprise by revealing that indeed we are already writing a book together. Instead I watch you, immersed in your universe, building a dream boat, before I pick up my pen and return to my dream of words.

Before sleep, cotton swab in hand, I paint each blister with the prescribed red tincture that promises to assuage the itch. I blow on them. I paint your face and the rest of your body in dozens and dozens of red polka dots that make you look like a glowing amanita mushroom. Tonight, you take longer than usual to fall asleep. I do not hear yawns or see the habitual fidgeting or eye-rubbing. Your gaze remains open, resisting the weight of sleep, hanging on to any thread of light that weaves under the door gap and the window shutters. I dare to open one eye to check how far you are along the road of dreams. You are staring at my face, eyes bright, present, and adoring.

"I love you, Papá," you say, pressing my face between your palms.

I am as touched as any human heart can be touched.

Then you sing:

I love you forever
I like you for always
As long as I'm living
My papá you'll be

This is a song from a favourite Canadian book on your shelf about a mother singing to her son throughout his childhood. She sang the song as he lay asleep, unaware of his mother's loving watchfulness, even into his adulthood when he visited and until the tables of caretaking turned. Then the son sings it to his mother through her older years while she sleeps…until death arrives to separate them. The song is carried onward as the son sings it to his daughter at bedtime, just as he had been sung to.

I do not have a memory of voicing the word *love* to my father in the many nights he stayed up worrying about my childhood illnesses, which were many. The mutual devotion lived between us, yet the words were never found. My father and I lacked the initiative to carve our own love language, even though he is among the gentlest of men in his generation anybody could encounter. As an adult, I write letters to my father and my mother about my love for them, especially when I am about to return to Canada. I leave the letters tucked under the pillow so they will read them the night I leave while I float over the Arctic ice. The words stand as a link in a culture and a family that did not build stronger bridges of demonstrative tenderness into adulthood.

Tonight your stamina returns, and aside from the myriad of blisters turned to crusts on your face, scalp, and torso, it is as if you are invincible again. Tonight you and I not only play-wrestle but also exchange massages and kisses. We tickle, and we caress. Since attending kindergarten in the Cambra valley for our winter sojourn, you also wish to play at punching and sword-fighting. I decline such play, much to your disappointment. I am aware that you will face aggressive people and personal-boundary trespassers throughout life. Sharpening your fighting skills to hold them off is the preferred response in our Hollywood-induced mythology. The will of the strongest fist or fastest gun dictates the outcome: respect. You will eventually witness plenty of fists, bullets, and axes staining TV screens red. And in real life, you will likely experience the power of knuckles bruising your skin. It is the world most men have created and perpetuated. I will not, though I am a man and a father. I want to postpone that exposure to the universe of violence, until you realize that there are alternatives, that manhood is not a sentence of violence. Aggression will not be playful when it arrives.

After a two-week Easter break you have recovered, despite the polka-dotted face and a scar on your cheek marking you on the same spot where I earned mine, also from chickenpox—except our scars are on the mirror side of each other.

At the school gate, you blow me a kiss. I twitch as if surprised by its flight landing on my cheek. I smile and send you mine express delivery, which apparently travels off target; luckily for me, you lunge to catch it, sticking it on your cheek with glee. We laugh.

When I meet up with you later that day, you come running into my arms. You call me Paulo, leaving a grandfather stupefied by hearing a child calling a father by name. You have been calling me by my name since your first words. I like it that you swing back and forth between my name and *papá*. We are father and son, and much more.

On school grounds, we cross paths with your uncle Filipe fetching your cousins Tomás and Simão for their music and martial arts lessons. You step forward to hug your uncle.

He tells you, "Men do not hug."

You keep your arms open, wanting to hug regardless.

"Men shake hands," he insists and stretches his hand.

You shrug. He cannot convince you. You cannot convince him.

"Give me five then."

You give him five.

You gaze at the surrounding hills the way I used to as a child. High hills and narrow horizons.

We begin our bedtime routine. I sit on the toilet to pee, then you do. You still do not imagine any other way to pee. I turn the bathtub tap on. The gurgle and thunder echoes in the white-tiled bathroom. We brush our teeth. Make faces at the mirror.

"I would like to have my hair long like Mamā and Amari."

You do not remember your hair uncut and long until the age of three, prompting many to call you a girl and you to correct them, but not always. You, too, enjoy ambivalence.

"Nice. At one time, I had hair reaching to my bum." I turn around and use my hand to mark the exact length.

When I visited your grandparents, Aunt Marina braided my hair in the morning while we sat in the sun by the portico stairs nibbling on tangerines, soaking up the warmth and listening to the blackbirds' morning notes sprinkling from the cedar tree.

You look at my shaved head in the mirror, show a puzzled face. The leap from braid to baldness is too large to fathom.

"What do you think of my hairstyle now?"

You look at it politely. "Nice. It would be even nicer if you had hair," you say with a confident nod of authority.

I laugh, test the temperature of the bathwater with one hand, turning the tap off with the other.

We undress.

Tonight you soap my face, and I soap yours. You want to learn to shave, and I let you run a bladeless shaver along my face. You are careful, bite your lip as you concentrate on plowing the snow-like foam from my face. In turn, you shiver in delight when I run my plastic shaver blade side up, and mow the foam from your skin. I run my hand over your cheek. "Smooth." You beam with pride and accomplishment. You have accomplished your first shave, and in your eyes you are now a man.

In bed that night, after the "What did you like best about today?" exchange and the usual serving of bedtime stories, you run your finger along my nose, across my eyebrows, and say, "One day I'll be a papá."

in search of spring

In search of spring, we stroll up the neighbourhood lanes still bordered with terraced farm fields, adjacent to houses and irrigation channels in this Portuguese countryside. Spring arrives earlier and earlier in the Cambra valley, although in fewer colours, floral geometries, and scents, the result of disappearing fields of corn and grapevines replaced by the crushing squareness of buildings. Energized by this ritual of spring I have not enacted since my childhood, I explain to your attentive four-year-old hazel eyes that we will collect these wildflowers to give our respective godmothers, and I save the surprise for you when a week later they return the affection by giving us sugar-coated almonds.

After gathering a bunch of flowers, you stare at the bundle in your hand.

"If we pick every flower, spring will not arrive and the bees will have no food." Your logical concern about the long-range consequences of a flower-picking ritual is better articulated than many an environment minister's resource extraction policy.

"Luckily it's only us picking flowers in this whole city, Koah."

You are not aware that most children now offer their godparents supermarket-bought flowers that parents have selected on their behalf.

"We shall only take a few flowers of each," I assure you.

The sun highlights a colony of stunted daisies drooping from the edge of a slope, prepared to jump from an abandoned field hemmed in by a crumbling stone wall. Out of a crevice in the loose wall hang the tiny white pearls from a flower we cannot name, yet we admire its delicate petals resting on our fingertips. We carry on, find tiny purple violets. This is Ti Fernanda's favourite flower, which inspired her to knit a dress in its colours for your sister, Amari. The purple of the petals filling the upper torso, the green of the leaves from the waist down, and the yellow of the pistil settled over the heart. For her finishing touches, she sewed on wooden flowers and rabbits.

A few steps further along the slope of this abandoned field, we find wild strawberry flowers. We leave those flowers untouched for others to savour the fruit in the summer. Instead, we pick daisies, lupine, dandelion, and a dozen more flowers of many a tint to join the palette of colours in our hands. Our fingers are stained yellow, brown, sprinkled with pollen. We smell spring in the pores of our skin.

Long-dormant grasses and undesired seeds tussle with the wind for a share of the sun among blooms once called weeds. The cycles of colour and scents carry onward outside human will. The orange beaks of *melros* stitch the sky in their flight and reassure us that for one more year the blue firmament will not cease to exist or even collapse upon us. Looking at the birds, we are reassured the sky will also haul the sun across its blue fields for another season of bountiful crops. The jay, song thrush, finch, and nightingale agree; they have returned to the fields in larger numbers than observed in my teenage years. Even abandonment brings its surprises, and land left to itself grows less tainted with the unwanted aid of pesticides that poison seeds, fruit, geckos, ladybugs, worms, and grasshoppers. This less destitute ecosystem will bring us a healthier menu and, who knows, perhaps longer lasting memories too.

A woman across the lane paces the perimeter of her courtyard, following our flower-gathering and talking to herself. Three large outbuildings hold racing pigeons and occupy most of her backyard. We are well acquainted with these pigeons released from their cubicles every late afternoon into the neighbourhood's sky. They fly above us as we feed collards to the goats on Ti Fernanda's farm. Ribbons of grey swoosh the air with joyful loops and sweeps, emitting a loud and pleasant sound of cavorting. These are the winged joggers of the clouds. Fat blue letters against the white walls of the pigeon outbuildings announce the years this family of birds have been long-distance national champions: 2009, 2010, 2011.

The woman pacing the perimeter no longer notices the cooing of her husband's pigeons, nor the fat letters on the building. Her gaze clings to you, Koah, and your chirps of joy as you discover a new type of flower to add orange and more scent to the miniature bouquet in your hand. You jump up and down in the lane to share the discovery. The woman dares herself, opens the metal gate—opens yet dares not step out. She repeats the refrain, "What a nice boy, what a nice boy." I wonder if there is an echo of a forgotten past in her life that prompts her smile, a smile not easily found in her pacing days. Her hands shake in the manner of your grandmother Micas. I wonder if, from her childhood, she remembers this wildflower ritual of Easter. I am tempted to bring her the tiny bundle of wildflowers in my hand. And I do. There is a mixture of sadness and desperation even in her smile and in the racing of her unintelligible words.

An old world of flowers and greenery has been long abandoned on the edge of the neglected fields and now they attempt to jump off. There is nowhere else to escape the moat of asphalt, cement walls, and ten times more houses lining the lanes. The daisies continue to peek from their precipice, cling to the edges between the wall's stones.

I gather a new bundle of flowers; you expand yours as the woman continues to follow us with her penetrating gaze. We tie the small posy with a stray stalk of rye from the ditch. Year after year, this small gesture also ties the affections and relationships in a family a little stronger. Later in the afternoon, you will give your bundle to your aunt Marina. I will give mine to my aunt Fernanda. On Easter Sunday, a week from now, our godmothers will give us a transparent cellophane pouch of multicoloured sugar-covered almonds. They resemble a bag of tiny bird eggs.

Once our voices fade as we turn the bend and return to Grandma's house down the lane, Alzheimer's will remain the company this neighbour woman knows. She paces the walled yard to the song of racing pigeons cooing, her gaze following us from inside her gate and as far as the perimeter wall will allow. Last week, I brought her husband an escaped canary that sought asylum in your grandparents' yard. It landed on the red and sun-warmed tiled steps of the kitchen portico where I sat reading only minutes before walking up the hill to meet you after school. The green- and yellow-feathered canary hopped around my feet, swooped near my head, peeked at my book. Without food in the wild, you, little canary, were deemed to perish. I returned you to captivity. The man thanked me, said it was the third time you had attempted a flight to freedom. Did I misunderstand you, dear bird?

Your grandmother Micas grows holy grass and rosemary sheltered by the waist-high cement wall. Once, oak woods began past that wall that now separates us from the first 1970s estate development of thirty houses, thirty feet below. You grandmother grows these scented herbs for a rite of Easter and breaks twigs from the rosemary bush into a bucket. Beside her, teeth clenched, you tug until a handful lets go, nearly making you fall backwards into the potato plant rows. You raise the holy herb leaves high and proud, a small hand dotted with chickenpox blisters and scabs, a small Christ in your own right.

Side by side with your grandmother Micas, you scatter a green carpet of scents at the iron gate to welcome the priest. The aromatic herbs will also mark the pathway up the red tiled steps to the dining room porch. Senhora Delfina, in the house across from our back entrance, scatters rose petals at her wooden gate. Your hands will hold onto the pleasant aroma for the rest of the day. The wind frustrates your intention to mark every step of the way with the greenery. You mumble your irritation and raise your gaze to the skies. This is not the first time you are unimpressed with the uncooperating elements of nature or of God. It will not be the last.

You return to join your first and second cousins kicking a football in the yard. Once in a while, the game stops; everyone listens to the miniature church bell travelling in the neighbourhood housing estate, announcing the priest and his party of four helpers carrying a golden cross, holy water, and the smudging incense from house to house. You are a band of six children excited by this religious ritual, monitoring their progress until minutes later, realizing they are now climbing up the lane, you erupt in a race into the house.

The priest, a young seminarian, walks in first and blesses the house, the dwellers, the walnut furniture, the bone porcelain, the blue and yellow Arraiolos tapestries, delivering a prayer with the sign of the cross. The actual gold cross follows inside the room, as large as a rabbit, much larger than a Kinder egg, brought around the half moon of people for everyone to kiss the bleeding feet of Jesus. There is no better way to pass around a plague. When it is placed in front of your face, you let the cross and the bloodied nailed feet hover in the uncomfortable collective silence. No one comments on your red chickenpox wounds and no one offers to kiss them, which may seem unfair when everybody bends to kiss the painted wounds on the doll. The suffering expression of the man on the cross does not pass unnoticed, and you must wonder about the meaning behind this sombre ceremony. Prompted and pressured by others to follow the expectation, prompted by the voice of your mother, you consent by pretending to kiss the bloodied feet nailed to the cross. Not fully pleased, the sacristan moves on to the next, a believer who will touch lips to feet, a less hesitant actor following the script.

I smile to you and nod. I hope you continue to watch and evaluate before blindly joining a social practice when it comes to smoking and drinking, be it wine or blood, real or metaphorical. It will serve you well. I am the last to have the crucifix brought before me, and I, too, do not kiss the feet. I wink at you. You smile.

When the sacristan reaches into his bag and offers you chocolate Easter eggs, you do not hesitate in accepting them. Your priorities are clear. You chose chocolate over religion, still unaware that chocolate bunnies are also a religion of the mercantile type. It is the newest, most compelling, and addictive religion for children your age. The wheel of history continues to impose the rituals of the conqueror upon the conquered as once the Romans brought their gods to the Iberian pagans, and later Christ merged with their goddess Ostara. Two millennia later, the Christian faith shows signs of crumbling as old deities cannot compete with the universal appeal of Cadbury and Nestlé. These modern gods are less interested in your spiritual salvation and set their sights on conquering the mind that commands the wallet. The older gods are waning, trampled by Walt Disney bunny hops and neon colours that draw every pupil to their pocket.

The magic of Ostara saving a wounded bird by turning it into a rabbit and in thankful appreciation receiving an egg is now mostly a forgotten story that gave rise to Easter Bunny lore. Other ancient stories from Egypt to Japan, often forgotten, mark a season of fertility, renewal, the triumph of light over darkness, good over evil, celebrating a season of eggs and representing the return of the sun and the cycles of rebirth.

After the blessing formalities, the priest tells the fourteen of us around the table that we have set an attendance record for their house-blessing circuit. "Like the old times," he said, not from experience but from storytelling lore. In my youth, every household opened its doors to the priest. Today a minority will partake in this door-to-door ritual, and even fewer will believe in it or understand its origin. The student priest notes this is the only house offering a bowl of old-fashioned sugar-covered almonds. We are a relic of the past, although your grandmother no longer has the stamina or emotional impetus to fill the table with half a dozen cakes baked amid the spring cleaning whirlwind of the previous day. She no longer covers the table with smoked meats, sausages, *presunto*, goat and sheep cheeses, quince marmalade and fig jams, or seasonal sweet breads such as *regueifas* and *pão de ló*, a sponge cake with its excess of eggs and sugar beaming its sunny glow inside and out—one of the many convent-sourced sweet recipes in the region, known for its decadent ingredients, a source of high bliss in the house of God, where the pleasures of sugar replaced the forbidden ones of sex. At your grandmother's Easter table, port, green, and burgundy wines also awaited the priest in the refuelling station of their overindulgent Calvary. Such were the bountiful tables of yesterday that invited the church to feast.

Today is not that once upon a time when the parish priest would walk the neighbourhood himself with his sacristans. This is not an era when time still exists, sanctioning the gods and their ambassadors to sit down and try the different culinary treats specific to each family's kitchen, while sitting for a ten-minute conversation. Today the parishioners' priest already walks with difficulty down the pulpit stairs to offer communion, dragging along his arthritic leg. Resurrection is not expected. The parish resorted to renting a priest to do the visiting. The waning impetus of life parallels the fading meaning of this socio-religious ritual in the lives of your grandparents, who go through its motions as another set of tasks to overcome without breaking a hip. The practical worries of life have also waned, so your grandmother is no longer tense at the prospect of the blessed water sprinkled into this formal dining room and landing on her velvet beige sofa, staining it forever. The velvet sofa has survived decades of Easter visits, and since it is never sat on, it will outlast all of us.

The priest takes his leave, wishing us a fruitful year brimming with health and prosperity. He scans the room, notices the many children and your baby sister. "May we all be here next year." He pauses to smile. "Perhaps even more of us," he adds, emphasis on the *more*, for indeed it is spring and the season of eggs and fertility, although not for him, according to present Catholic church rules, which priests have no vote on or hope to change themselves. Everyone laughs until your nine-year-old cousin, Tomás, quips, "Or less of us."

This sober thought brings a pained look to both your grandparents and an uneasy silence that I break. "We will certainly be less. We will be in Canada next Easter." I imagine your cousin's words reflected a natural counterpoint, reminding us of an uncertainty everyone should expect, a reminder of the higher odds of death that Easter also celebrates. I applaud the remark and might have said it myself in more spontaneous and courageous times in my life. Your aunt Marina has told me Tomás attends catechism class half-heartedly and is perhaps already plotting his first boycott of religion through his incisive questions.

The priest's party marches onward to the next house. Their small talk, rethreaded over the years and lanes, drifts up the stairs, reweaves the interrupted daylong futebol arguments that ease the purgatory of the day. These spirited futebol concerns are far more common to every contemporary Portuguese household, and find an echo in your uncle Filipe's earlier comment to the sacristan about your sister Amari's misguided wardrobe choice; her matching burgundy and red frill outfit celebrate the colours of his archenemy football club and not the blues and whites of his own. The men laughed their expected laugh. As soon as the band leaves our iron gate, the story of our parish priest who loved the blood of Christ more than Christ himself returns to the table conversation, a story I heard three decades earlier—a sign that good stories are no longer as bountiful. The adults move to the kitchen and sit staring at the screen they had left talking to itself minutes before.

The echo of the sacristan's bell moving along the lane still reaches us, and I run to the yard with the children, where we will begin a beloved ritual of your generation. The thick granite walls of the Old World faiths are crumbling, and the limber rabbits have hopped over the rubble to evangelize the young minds with new bottom-line concepts ruled by numbers, additions, and first addictions. The bunnies, effervescent and screeching, bring hedonism not penance, pleasure, not pain. Your first Easter egg hunt is officially on. In the yard, while we sniff for the imaginary eggs of rabbits, we become the new hounds raised on sugar. Above us, the nesting blackbirds chirp their complaint to the deaf ears of excited children dreaming of oval-shaped happiness. The blackbirds shuttle back and forth from the imported cedar tree, where they are guarding a nest and may have already hatched their eggs.

Easter Sunday ends with games of hide-and-seek, the hyper screeches of joy a far cry from the self-flagellation and crucifixion the season celebrates. Your darkened palms and sticky moustache conceal the red of the calamine tincture. They resemble the humus of the earth, but not exactly. What appears to be one thing is often another in this world of representations, and so you commune with the grass, where you collapse next to your cousins in sugar burnout, staring at the sky.

"Children, it is getting colder," your grandfather Agosto calls from the kitchen, already wearing a brown coat. Your gaze follows the first flight of a bat scooping insects from the twilight. It swerves among the criss-cross of birds sharing the sky for the last crumbs of the day, encouraged by the chirping of their hungry young. "Children, you'll get a cold in this evening dew." You resist more calls to move inside, unwilling to release a day in the presence of a larger family that makes this world a less lonely place.

You savour the last moments of the day reverberating through your body, the sun entering your pupils to bring the whole body aglow. Your cousins retreat inside. You want your story to last a little longer. You stay and stare at Sirius, the first star of the falling night.

enclosures

By the hand of your great-uncle Zé and great-aunt Fernanda, you and your sister, Amari, enter the enormous bird enclosure. The cackle begins. The geese do what they do best: warn those inside and those one hundred metres around the farm that intruders have arrived. The sound is deafening. The peacocks join the chorus. You inspect the clay roost lined with straw, where the chickens lay their eggs.

"How many, Koah?"

You shrug, disappointed. There are none to collect.

The daily visits to the farm and to the animals offer you a type of informal schooling that no longer exists elsewhere in this neighbourhood. You are the last student of this farmland, entering the pens, cages, coops to play with the animals, or running across the fields to inspect the bugs that hide under scattered implements.

No other child is seen holding a ladybug on the palm of a hand, or sticking twigs into the mole's underground tunnels, hoping to stir one out of its hide-and-seek game.

In these five months in Portugal, you are becoming fluent in more than another human language to aid you in relating with different cultures. You are also learning to converse with the animals, the trees, and the stones. You are listening to those who will soon be killed and eaten and learning about the violence of the world. This is a place where the pigs hang by their hind legs, splayed at the spine like crimson books in butcher windows. At the end of our road, the suckling ones are a delicacy on a spit. The price of one euro per kilo is offensively low for a life, if there ever was a fair price for death.

Great-uncle Zé walks you around the little cement pond. Ducks race in laps, motored by their orange paddles, pretending it is not another typical day of mayhem. The blend of mud and fowl droppings, its squish, squish, arrests your steps. You stare at your once flashy green runners. Sighing, you carry on. The raft of ducks makes no waves until you arrive at the rectangular wooden birdhouse on stilts, home to the Pekin bantams. Then the ducks also quack up their own storm. You crawl and disappear inside the deep and narrow henhouse too short even for your four years. Moments later, you hold a tiny bantam egg. Your palm opens and closes, feeling the small frail shell.

The striking white feathers of the pheasant distract us from the ruthless beak that last week killed a helmeted guinea fowl and a peacock several times his size. The strong farm arms of your great-uncle Zé lift you to where, balanced and woven against a grapevine, baby pigeons chirp in their nest.

"We leave those babies be, Koah," Uncle Zé tells you, as your hand stretches out to touch the nest.

Iridescent in the light, the nest shines from the blue-green peacock feathers collected to decorate it. The mother pigeon flies frenetically about the enclosure. Other pigeons fly in and out through the small gaps in the wire ceiling. These are racing pigeon refugees from the neighbour, birds no longer capable of earning their keep in medals or pride. They now seek shelter, easy food, and company amid the larger family of winged ones.

This is the same uncle who decades ago invited me and the neighbourhood children for an afternoon of killings in the orchard. Hosts of sparrows had been pecking at the cherries, irritating him and other neighbours also at war with the hungry birds competing for their favourite fruits.

I remember wounded sparrows, wings broken by shots of the pellet gun, flapping sideways on the grass. I remember sparrows missing eyes, frozen in shock, blood trickling down their necks, the soft grey feathers in my hand staining red. I have never stopped remembering.

I stayed at a distance as the other houndlike boys raced after the fired shot and fetched the wounded creature, who remained very still in the grass, stunned by fright, pain, or by the smell of death. The boys collected the quasi-dead sparrows and strung them by the feet, twenty to a twine, a cascade of death that hung from a post as a warning to other winged creatures. Including their ineffective guardian angels.

The neighbourhood boys and your great-uncle Zé proceeded to pluck the feathers from the tiny sparrows after they had been immersed in the stockpots of boiled water. This was the boys' initiation into a mass killing that apparently had been a pastime in your great-uncle's childhood, using the crude slingshot technology of their era. He sang the praises of the delicacy to come as a reward for the hard work of the afternoon soldiers: a well-earned tomato rice bird stew. I remained a little behind the eager boys, chopping onions. My lips were clenched.

During the extended dinner preparation, your great-uncle Zé entertained the boys with tales of ambushes, exotic snake attacks, and night guerrilla battles during his time in a West African war, one of the bloodiest Portuguese colonial battles. Within fourteen years, in Guinea-Bissau, ten thousand conscripted soldiers lost their lives, and one hundred thousand Africans lost theirs. Many young Portuguese men fled the country to avoid the draft. Your underaged great-uncle Zé was an eager early volunteer, later returning with a *love* tattoo for his regiment on his forearm.

When the dinner call arrived, I did not sit at the long table of twelve. Hearing the tiny bird bones crunching inside the joyful mouths of the other children served as the conclusion to that story. That was the afternoon I became a non-meat eater in my mind, although it took two more decades before it became daily practice.

The goats bleat; they recognize your voice in the distance and anticipate the vegetable compost peels we will scatter on the ground amid their stampede. When we arrive, they prop their front legs against the wooden gate slats in the corral, their necks craned for first choice. After their compost feast, you allow the two lambs to lick your fingers. Their serrated teeth tickle your skin, you say. The wool on their bodies still shines white, unlike their parents' coats, dirt-grey from the permanent straw-dust cloud in the windowless cement enclosure.

We climb the knoll to the upper fields where the goats await. In heat, the buck reeks. My eyebrows rise. You do not seem to mind the gallant's choice of perfume. The goats press their bodies to the double wire fence that cannot prevent their heads from squeezing through. They stretch their tongues to reach for the deep green collard in your hand. After an hour of back and forth snapping collard leaves from the field, you lie down on the grassy ditch next to the fence and converse with the four-legged. I cannot hear what you say. Goats stare and listen, despite the lack of collard in your hands. Once in a while, the large male or the baby bleats. A fence separates.

You are learning about the imprisonments that condition the free movement of beings and how a prison also conditions the guards, who can never live far from the fences themselves. One day, you will learn that this profession is still called husbandry, a practice rooted in domesticating and controlling the lands and its non-human creatures. And one day, a little or a lot later, you may choose to have a woman companion that convention will call a wife. Then you may want to question the links, the meanings *encooped* in these words, in these practices, and you may also choose not be husband to a wife. Or a husband to a husband.

Once a week, your cousins Tomás and Simão join us in our many stopovers, as we stroll back home from your school. We run a leaf-boat race in the irrigation channel, followed by a soy yogurt snack at your grandparents'. The afternoon then wraps up with a visit to the farm, next door at Ti Fernanda's. We visit the animals in their enclosures; we harvest tangerines or clementines; we take time to play with puppy Bolinhas, the friendly Labrador, tossing him the squeaky rubber ball.

You convince your reticent older cousins to join your goat-feeding adventures. At first, they remain behind. You grin, showing off your comfort before four-legged creatures who are taller than you, for this is a rare territory where you are more proficient than they are. Soon, Tomás and Simão join in feeding collards to the goats, allowing the fast mouths to snap the stalks from their hands. Joyously, you jump, understanding what you have accomplished.

Two days later while you feed the goats collard leaves, your great-aunt Fernanda arrives with a glimmer in her eye. "Come." You giggle and follow her; you appreciate surprises. It takes all your might to control the pace of your steps and remain behind your great-aunt. In the kitchen, by the fireplace, sits a shoebox. Ti Fernanda opens it. *Piu...piu...* Your eyes widen to the fluffy chick inside, born just hours ago. The bird cowers and attempts to hide in the corner of the shoebox.

"You can pick her up, Koah," great-aunt Fernanda encourages.

You are not so sure. "Where's the mamma?"

"It doesn't have a mamma."

You do not believe her.

A dish, the size of a jar lid, has overturned inside the shoebox, scattering gritty cornmeal feed. The bird burrows under the thin layer of wood shavings cushioning the shoebox.

Your great-aunt cups her hands, lifts the chick up. The bird attempts to jump. A fall on the hard tile could break her tooth-pick-thin legs. Ti Fernanda passes the bird to your cupped hand. Your index finger runs over the bald and bony head no larger than your thumb, then caresses the yellow fuzz on her wing. A combination of tenderness and awkwardness, since the bird wants to walk out of your hand, and you are unsure how to handle this fragility asserting her own will.

After a time, the fast-pulsing chest suggests a stressed bird. I propose walking outside to see the goats. You stay a moment longer, kneeling by the box, watching.

"The bantam chickens brooded on this egg, as they will on any egg sneaked into their roost, Koah," Ti Fernanda says, before continuing on, explaining that they will not care for the chick once hatched, realizing only then the fledging is not theirs.

I smile. Your great-aunt tricks the bantams in order to increase her stock of chickens and consequently must attend to the motherless chicks.

The next day, outside your hearing range, your great-uncle Zé, wearing his morning stubble like frost in a field, whispers to me that the chick nearly died. That morning, they found her lifeless in the shoebox. The spring night had been colder than usual. About to toss the chick in the garbage bin, he lifted the cold body and placed it back in the box next to the morning fire. After an hour, the *piu... piu...* of the chick caught his attention. She was on her feet and eager to eat.

I did not tell you this story when you raced into the kitchen that afternoon to hold the chick in your palm, talking to her with the tenderness of a father loving his own offspring.

Another day has passed. I steer you to the goats' fenced field and avoid walking near the kitchen. Your great-uncle Zé tells me the chick dehydrated, forgotten in front of the heater.

When you ask about the newborn chick, I mumble about it not being in the kitchen any longer. You know it is an excuse, yet you ask nothing more. There is another side to your great-aunt and great-uncle that you do not yet see or understand. It is a paradoxical equation of affections. For all the incommensurable love Ti Fernanda and Ti Zé show you, there is also their unconscious side, in neglecting their farm animals. I don't know why I believe I must wait for another time to explain best the unintended or intended cruelty of those who are close to us. The most difficult affections, you will learn, are when love and harm intersect. Some of your deepest hurts in memory will likely come from me, since I have already provided you with your first disappointments, aggravations, and conflicts.

Sometimes those who love us are willing to listen, and even willing to change because of the emotional gravitational pull we have on their lives. Your grandfather Agosto stopped caging birds after a few years of listening to my unhappiness at seeing the birds in captivity. I suggested he could also enjoy them flying about in the sky and yard. He would fall silent and stare at the caged birds. One day I arrived from Canada to find the bird enclosures not only empty but also dismantled.

"They are never far, anyway," he told me, pointing out a nest in the tall ornamental cedar beside us. In the ensuing quiet, the chirping of baby *melros* trickled down. Soon, a mother darted in with a wriggling worm on her beak.

Your grandfather smiled.

At the age of nine, I attempted to keep birds, to emulate and please your grandfather Agosto and his father, both following a multigenerational family tradition. I was given a breeding pair of pigeons and reminded that it was a serious responsibility to look after their well-being. The pigeons were free to come and go from a wooden birdhouse propped high, next to your other great-grandfather Matos's bedroom window. The birds disappeared after the first week. They never returned. Some children on the lane said they were stolen; others said they were eaten. The pigeons might have simply opted to fly to freedom. I will never know. I was saddened. Inside I carried the weight of their disappearance and the conclusion that I had been incapable of caretaking. Never again did I wish to keep birds.

On arriving in Portugal, you cringed upon seeing chained dogs barking frantically from their tiny cement doghouses. "Why does Ti Zé tie them up? Why is that second dog barking so madly at me?" After a few weeks, you have begun to accept their neurotic condition and to imitate your great-uncle, who taught you to use an osier twig to strike Bolinhas, eliciting compliance for sitting and rolling on the lawn.

There is a tale of two chained dogs on your great-uncle Zé's farm. Bolinhas, a recently acquired puppy, lives in a cement doghouse next to the raven's now-empty cage. This Labrador belongs to Ti Zé's granddaughter, who lives in Brussels. She requested a puppy to play with twice a year on her Christmas and summer visits. Willing to please his granddaughter, Ti Zé unchains Bolinhas to run off-leash in the yard most days and feeds him store-bought dog food and treats, while the twelve-year-old mutt Caima, two chain lengths away on the other side of the fence, looks on and sniffs the drifting air. His bones mimic the ribcage of a disintegrating caravel. Never off his chain, Caima watches from the adjacent muddy field. Any time we bring the veggie scraps from grandmother Micas's house to feed Ti Fernanda's sheep, we also carry a bowl of leftover soup, chicken bones, and day-old cornbread for Caima. He yaps and wags his tail. It is not every day we have leftovers.

You are learning about human incoherence, witnessing that some affections are narrow, selective, leaving the heart blind to others. It is a roulette of fortune. The ball seldom lands twice on the same lucky number. That is why when the sun shines on us, it is essential to be grateful for privilege and not be blinded by self-absorption. In those moments, it is kind to look around, seeking those who need the warmth and have been confined to the shadows.

Ti Zé and Ti Fernanda are not conscious of the harm they inflict on animals, having been born into farming practices carried out for centuries. The absence of day-to-day moral dissent also permits unchallenged behaviour to flourish. You and I are also at the mercy of our cultural blindness, and it is our obligation to peel away such blinds to make our choices free from obvious social and cultural conditioning. You hold significant emotional influence over those around you, as they are willing to hear and please you. They want your happiness and will expand that circle of care to others, if you so insist.

I encourage you to speak your worries about the chained dogs to Ti Zé.

You do.

He laughs.

You don't.

Ti Zé does not know what to tell you. It is the way he has lived his life with farm animals. By domination. Punishment. Their servitude. He once shot his dog in anger for biting him when he struck the dog with a hose for having disobeyed a command. It will take another trillion raindrops to change the shape of a stone that believes its present form is all it can be. Patience is the most difficult practice for those who do not have a thousand years to live, those witnessing animals already dying every day from neglect and abuse. Patience is difficult for those of us recognizing another's pain.

Day after day, following the slowness of the seasons, you have already grown to understand the necessary courage to make this world a better place. Yet the one who names the injustice while standing among those benefitting from that injustice becomes vulnerable, often triggering redirected wrath.

I look forward to you growing older, even more articulate and assertive, and bringing to light the numerous, varied enclosures in my mind. I hope to be grateful while dismantling such mental cages, to free the dreams still invisible to me. That day will mark the beginning of another journey, one more reciprocal, in the learning exchange between us.

It is our last week in the valley, and you are turning stones on a field, looking for worms, finding snails instead, which you roll on your hand to inspect.

When you attempt to separate a snail from its shell, I explain that the snail will die without it, and since it is attached, it would likely be as painful as tearing your arm from your body. You move your attention on to the glistening black slugs in collard paradise. From a wooden ladder propped against the roof tiles on the herb-drying building, I harvest sweet-smelling tangerines. I have only collected a dozen tangerines in the bag when you arrive.

"Paulo, Paulo."

In your hand, you hold a tiny snail. Its broken shell reveals a hole the size of your thumb. Your face tells me that you are upset.

"Will it die?"

"It might. A shell doesn't grow back. Small and fragile creatures depend on our gentleness."

You become silent, staring at the snail you have returned to the ground. It is not moving.

I have seen or heard the stories of animals perishing on this farm. From territorial fowl that should not be sharing crowded enclosures to sheep without their water replenished on scorching days, from infirm ostrich, rabbits, or chickens to an ailing gaunt mare meeting her last moment, the plethora of agonies are endless.

The animals are ornamental objects Ti Fernanda and Ti Zé dream up for their vision of a farm. The creatures become living toys to entertain grandchildren and other visitors. Your great-aunt and great-uncle fail to see farm animals as feeling beings who suffer and require the love, attention, and care dispensed to you and your sister. Fernanda's and Zé's perennial struggle to remain within the limits of accomplishable farm tasks in a day costs these incarcerated creatures their lives. The animals cannot help themselves and will live or die at the mercy of an unreliable hand.

In Canada, your mother protested the mistreatment of farm, food, work, and entertainment animals well before it became more recognized and reported. On the street carrying banners, being spat on and insulted, she has stood for those without a say at any table, political or otherwise, or a place of equality in the conscience of most *sapiens*. You were only six months old when you marched with us in the kangaroo carrier to the beat of Mamma's samba band, protesting a crude pipeline that would destroy the habitat of wild animals and the living of Indigenous Peoples. But it would have been less safe for you to have joined her on the front lines of protest against horse carriages in Victoria.

You do not yet know that it breaks your mother's heart to walk onto this farm, yet she does not let her sadness diminish your joy in your interaction with the animals. This farm is a playpen for you, but an animal concentration camp for us.

Progress is being made. Demonstrating growing consciousness and sensitivity, many societies currently expect responsibility and accountability in relationships and interactions with other non-human sentient beings. They consider unnecessary harm or neglect inflicted on other creatures grounds for criminal charges, and so your great-aunt and great-uncle might be fined, or perhaps even jailed, were they living in a country such as Canada. Not so in Portugal. After all, this is a culture that promotes bullfighting as a reflection of national identity, and where torturing an animal has been a public enjoyment and an equestrian skill proudly displayed for centuries. As if tradition excused torture. It is during this winter stay that, for the first time, a Portuguese law is passed to stop killing shelter animals as a population reduction measure. The law was spearheaded in parliament by your second cousin Ana. Last year, Portugal also elected the first PAN Party parliamentarian. A party that stands for people, animals, and nature rights. The first sustained winds of change in animal welfare awareness have arrived.

Since childhood, Ti Fernanda and Ti Zé have been among my favourite aunt and uncle for their generosity, playfulness, spontaneity, and good disposition. Despite contradictions and our ethical and moral divergence, they continue to be dear to me as they already are dear to you. It is a tense cliff edge at times. They understand where my values clash with theirs. In our complex web of human and family affections, we hold this reality: a great-aunt and great-uncle who can be ignorant of the suffering they cause.

We teach you that this or any other farm's existence is not a validation, much less an endorsement, of an animal's natural fate.

Month by month, year by year, we will teach you to see beyond the veneer of appearances and to read between the lines, seeking the missing narratives. Ignorance can carry on for eternities, like sadness and its acceptance. How we treat vulnerable beings is an elemental matter to our higher consciousness and reflects our core selves. We will be defined not only by what we choose to create but also by what we refuse to destroy.

Today is April 25, Revolution Day. The Portuguese celebrate deposing a fascist government that ruled the country for forty years until 1974, the year Aunt Marina was born. I was nine years old. The image I retain most vividly replays: an old woman in black scurrying along the cobblestone road shouting, "The revolution has arrived, the revolution has arrived! Olive oil is going down to *cinco tostões* a bottle now, five cents. *Viva a Revolução!*" Olive oil's price increased every year thereafter. It is two hundred times more expensive today and no longer the cooking staple of the working people. It has been substituted in their kitchens by imported sunflower oil. Not only had the people become free that day, the market had also. The median wage has risen a mere fourteen times since that April day. More importantly, a myriad other essential gains, from education to health, have been achieved, and every citizen is free to complain now, meaning that political imprisonment or torture is no longer permitted.

This holiday afternoon, we prepare to visit the cousins from your grandfather's side of the family in the neighbouring county of Oliveira. Their semi-rural, three-house cluster holds nine people. Their extended clan across three generations of committed hobby farmers grows most of their vegetables and fruit, animal flesh and herbs.

Every year, our cousins effusively receive you and Amari. In fine Portuguese hospitality style, a banquet of home-baked sweet cakes and breads awaits us, including vegetarian dips and healthy options for the odd Canadians we are. They believe the non-meat inclination is a generalized Canadian trait, not our fringe family preference.

The cousins immediately take you and Amari to visit the two dozen rabbits they raise in cages. You pet them and their babies. No one tells you the rabbits are food. A dinner plate destiny for these long-eared fuzzy creatures does not cross your mind. When I look at those rabbits, a deep knot in my stomach reaches back to my childhood.

Every Saturday, I accompanied my father, often with my mother, to your great-grandfather Manuel da Costa's farm in the village of Vermoim, over the Cambra hills. That is where I met these second cousins weekly, and we played in terraced fields and backwoods.

Several times a year, I watched your grandfather Agosto kill and prepare a rabbit for the Sunday roast the following day, a special lunch to reward the long workweek.

On one of those Saturday afternoons, your grandfather selected the plumpest rabbit from the wooden cage and brought the buck dangling from hind legs to the cement washing tank. The water gurgled in a continuous stream, overflowing to a channel that irrigated the cornfields down below. In the past, some rabbits had squirmed and sprung, resisting what they must have smelled was their approaching end. Others dangled, resigned, or perhaps frozen in fear. Beneath the hanging pigeon house and the cooing birds, Vovô Agosto would hold the rabbit upside down. A swift hack of his hand to the rabbit's neck was as good as an axe. The

strike aimed to fracture the rabbit's spine, to instantly kill. Two
or three strikes sufficed.

The smack, smack, smack echoed against the tender splash of
water flowing from the black plastic pipe that brought cool water
from the spring on the hill, several hundred metres above. The two
pigeons stopped their cooing at the first strike of bone on bone.

With unease, I watched the fear in the rabbit's eyes intensifying
after the first strike, its springing legs attempting to hop away from
the nightmare, yet finding no ground beneath them. Your grandfather struggled to aim the next strike at the neck, made more
difficult by the wildly swinging rabbit in his grasp. He clenched
his lips, not enjoying the task.

After the third strike, the rabbit became motionless. Your
grandfather tied its hind legs with a cord and dangled the rabbit
from the two knobs on the double door. The soft white belly
faced us. A couple of quick slices along the heel revealed muscle, allowing a hold for your grandfather's fingers to pull off the
rabbit's fur coat in a steady, loud rip. The first tear echoed in
the still air of the hot afternoon as the rabbit began to violently
swing from the wall. The carpal bone strikes of the hand had
only stunned the rabbit to unconsciousness. I screamed. Your
grandfather turned pale.

"Stop. He is alive."

"They're only muscle spasms," your grandfather tried to
assuage me.

Blanch-faced, he continued ripping the fur to end everyone's
agony sooner. The rabbit stopped jerking after a few seconds, suc-
cumbing to the pain of being skinned alive, having woken up from
one horror to experience another far worse.

You cradle your cousin's rabbit against your chest. It kicks, wanting to hop away. The jostle frightens you. You move on to visiting the chickens and stomp in their fenced yard, attempting to catch one, cautioned not to step on their droppings. A car zooms past on the nearby road, and the song that symbolizes the revolution, played today on every radio and TV, drifts away with it. "Grândola, Vila Morena" always makes me think of your other great-aunt Fernanda, imprisoned and tortured while in the resistance movement, whose mental health, after release, was never the same. I had planned for you to finally meet her on this trip, while showing you Coimbra, the city of my university years; however, she died days before we landed, having choked on her breakfast, alone in the bedroom of her old age home.

We leave the chicken coop and stroll in the vegetable garden. Your Bustelo cousins tenderly lift you off the ground to reveal the three wild nests of *melros* and serin finches concealed among the dense foliage of their pear and apple trees. They leave them be.

After indulging in the afternoon feast disguised as a humble snack, we all stroll along a fallow field. A ladybug lands on your chest, a butterfly on your shoulder. You hold the ladybug on your open palm until it flies away. We soon say goodbye to our relatives, carrying home armfuls of arugula, lettuce, watercress, collards, cabbage, fresh lemon balm for tea, dill, and oregano. This green bounty will feed us for days.

On our return home from Bustelo, you want to squeeze in a visit to the goats and the sheep. Hoping to drop leftovers to Caima, you are disappointed when grandmother Micas says there are none today. The sun slides down the horizon, assailed by the cutting wind from the north. We are at the end of another Revolution Day.

My mention of returning to the apartment, a three-hundred-metre walk from Ti Fernanda's farm, prompts a sudden wave of tiredness, and you cannot drag one foot in front of the other.

I attempt to motivate you. "Tomorrow is the start of your last week in school, Koah."

"Paulo, school is boring. We sit most of the day."

I understand. For the first time in your life, you are experiencing entrapment. It is apartment life in winter, at the busiest intersection of this small city; it is the lack of lushly treed parks; but mostly it is the confinement to four walls in school for five weekdays. All of this is a new way of living after playing in the spacious green spaces, forests, and shores of Victoria. You want to escape walls as a bird wants to escape a cage.

You have not been conditioned to stillness, hypnotized by screens, or inured to confined living spaces. You want your day to continue in your grandparents' yard or your great-aunt's farm across the lane. *Domestication* is a word you have yet to learn, although you smell its approach. That is also why you do not sleep under a blanket. Even in your sleep, the lightest bedsheet covering you is kicked away. You want no pressure, no weight upon your dreams.

We stroll down to where the lane joins the larger road leading to our apartment. At the corner, in the house with many pets, the effusive parrot greets you. "Olá." You match his high-pitched screech with a returning "Olá." You stop, lean over the spiked railing to talk, and admire the bird scratching his grey feathery torso with his unchained leg. He walks sideways in frenetic steps along the stick perch, excited to see you, pleased with your attention. This parrot knows many a word you do not, vivid curses. He practises them on you. You are impressed that he can talk. As usual, you wish to visit longer than I am willing to stand in this sidewalk-less lane amid veering vehicles. The parrot is catching the last rays of the day, which highlight his red and green crest, before he returns to the kitchen, where he spends most of his life.

We finally begin moving again and are within sight of the apartment when we hear the cry of a bird in the sky. The insistent and long song accompanies the last droplets of light.

"Spring must be near, Koah."

That is when you begin singing:

Uma gaivota voava, voava,	*(A seagull flew, flew)*
asas de vento,	*(wings of wind,)*
coração de mar.	*(heart of the sea.)*
Como ela, somos livres,	*(Like her, we are free,)*
somos livres de voar.	*(we are free to fly.)*

My heart stops. You sing it freely and lightly. Acquainting you with the sounds of Portuguese while in the womb every night, I sang you this verse. I am surprised and unsure how you have memorized the words. You do not yet know the political context of this song. I sang you revolutionary freedom songs from '74 to welcome you into the world. What you do not yet know is that the people of Portugal borrowed the images of free animals, such as the gull in our ocean-kissed country, to inspire them to attain their own freedom. Now that the Portuguese people are freer than they were in my childhood, it is time to extend the favour to others who are not free: the animals still incarcerated in our midst.

Nearing the apartment, on our last week in the valley, you slow down our progress by first walking backwards, then testing your balancing skills and walking on the long thin wall of another apartment complex. You pretend to be an acrobat probing your limits. Then without warning, you jump down from the wall like the kid you are.

"We have to free the goats, Papá. Once we are gone to Canada, they need to be able to get the collards on their own."

"You are right, Koah. I'll let Ti Zé know."

"Please don't forget." You say it with your most serious face.

"I will certainly not."

You carry on along the wall, hopping up and down, until you stop and turn to me, full of conviction.

"And the chickens, too, need to be freed," you conclude, adding a determined nod.

It is another April, four decades after carnations plugged the barrels of machine guns, and the revolution is yet to arrive at the enclosures of those animals we have used as inspiration for action in art and song. We are the jail keepers and dictators we believed we had freed ourselves from. Perhaps the April revolution will mature alongside you and your sister, as you run through the sandy Furadouro beach and dive into the Atlantic, seeking the perfect surf. The wave will curl up, almost shy, just before unravelling its power. It will propel you far and wide. Then the seagulls, flying freely above the sailing boats, will join you, singing their song.

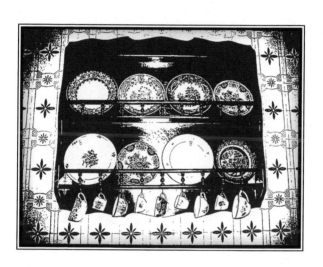

departures

The Sunday of our departure approaches as the land warms up and the heavy winter skies lift over the Cambra hills. The days stretch, and Portugal will be at its shiniest in another change of moon, beckoning your cousins Simão and Tomás, Aunt Marina, and Uncle Filipe to sandy beaches and mountain rivers for their communion with the waters, of which there are plenty. From the continuous massaging of the Atlantic on the rugged shores to the cascading rivers and streams weaving their pathways down the Freita hills, this romping rhythm will replace the less alluring refrain of water sliding off the grey skies.

After saying goodbye to your grandparents for the day, we slow down our steps to our apartment. For the first time, I point out to you the *Matos* in black lettering above the apartment entrance. "One of your four family names, Koah." This building was erected over your great-grandfather Manuel's cornfields and vineyards, his gift to his descendants, although he could not have anticipated the metamorphosis his fertile offering would take. Ten years after his death, a block of that land was exchanged for two apartments and a storefront for your grandparents.

Our open and scattered suitcases on the bedroom floor await your final decision on which toys to carry back and which to leave behind. You vacillate, negotiate, and finally accept that the guitar and the wooden train track set are not to travel. The plush toys and books, the board games, and puzzles line up next to the suitcases awaiting their fate, as if prepared to hop in at the flash of your hazel eyes.

There is a tinge of hurt in your cousins' eyes seeing our excitement during our packing preparations for a return to Canada. We hold two lives in our hearts. It goes beyond two languages and countries. We inhabit distinct universes that interweave unique values and practices, and this has taught us to navigate change in our lives with excitement. As birds shuttling in the sky, we migrate across mountain ranges and oceans to other lives and landscapes where we become others, sometimes unrecognizable. Your cousins Simão and Tomás have never left their familiar cultural borders and have always lived in the same building. Such permanence is a rare experience for a nine-year-old Canadian child.

"Why don't you just stay?" Tomás asks when no one else dares to.

"Our life is in Canada." I offer a vague answer, accompanied with a hug he shrugs away from.

I avoid discussing our reasons for not wanting to stay. I see the rejection in your cousin's face; a reflection that this Cambra valley, themselves, your teacher, and new school friends are not good enough to tip the balance of our affections. That life elsewhere is far better in order for us to sacrifice being away from family, which is the highest sacredness of Portuguese culture. If there is one thing I have learned and would like you to remember into adulthood, it is that no sacrifice is worth my well-being and fulfillment just so that I may carry on with an oppressive expectation or tradition in order to please a community. Yet there are many who, after a decade abroad, do return to their first homeland, able to build their dream houses and provide their children with a higher education in the same valley that neglected them.

Little by little, day by day, your cousins have watched in silence the suitcases filling up. Their bulky hulls will mostly carry hand-me-down clothes for you and your sister. Over the years, you have inherited your cousins' wardrobe. Tomás, who, like me, never has an easy time of letting go of anything he likes, offers you two of his Lego sets in addition to his favourite aviator game. Simão generously offers Noddy books, those he knows to be your favourites. We give them books and Canadian coins.

By the end of our extended visit, your cousins are more adept at dropping their *Skylanders* video game or Wii consoles and crossing the hallway to join us in playing our invented amusements. It's a significant change from the initial months when they were not interested in leaving their screens, and disappointed, you walked back to our apartment to play by yourself or with me, building wooden train tracks, solving puzzles, playing the electronic drum kit.

After dinner, your grandmother Micas arrives breathless and clacking her dentures, exhausted from the climb up the stairs to the apartment. She is carrying an offering: your favourite red grapes for dessert. She sits on my black office chair, her feet dangling, watching us pack the suitcases. For the month before our departure, your grandmother has been voicing her dread of the quiet to soon fill her old house. She will not have your exuberance arriving from school for your afternoon bread-and-cheese snack, your sister's rosy cheeks and chirps in the yard, the company of my late night conversations before I leave her to watch T V, avoiding the silences.

Every night before bed, your grandmother Micas will kiss your and Amari's picture on her bedside table. The cold glass frame resembles a touch of the snowy lands she has seen only once when I lived in the shadow of the Rockies. Although not voiced, although not made bare, the loss and the mourning uncovered by our departure becomes a foreshadowing of the more imminent disappearances impossible to deny in your grandparents' old age and frail health. "When will you return?" she asks even before you leave. You shrug, not knowing the answer.

In leaving, the hope of reunion is ever present. For five months, they saw you every day, often more than once. Your presence highlighted their loneliness. They emerged from their solitude, and the T V screen lost its altar-like status in your presence. This story was a gift of time for your grandparents, a gift they are yet to find the words to thank you for.

We will trigger a small death in many hearts, as the apartment building stairwell will no longer carry your excited screeches and daily rush down the steps to hide, followed by a "Boo-wooo, I'm here," all wrapped and bow-tied by your jovial laughter.

Your grandmother Micas will fall into a little depression when she comes to visit your aunt Marina and cousins in the building, as the closed heavy wooden door of our apartment stops her heart like a sealed coffin lid. In the five months we spent here, your cries, banter, and Noddy, Panda, and Pocoyo songs seeped under the apartment door, echoing up and down the stone stairwell for everyone to hear. This has been the most compressed living I have experienced since I was eighteen years old in a Coimbra university commune. For us, the departure will also be a small death, although the family left behind and carrying on in this valley must move among the empty spaces and the silences made more visible by our absence. In the same way that we already miss the fifteen-metre oak tree we had relied on for shade and company in Ti Fernanda's farmyard, now chain-sawed to chunks in a corner, sacrificed for firewood.

On your last school day, your teachers and your classmates organize a farewell celebration. They create a personalized yearbook highlighting the best photos and mementos, though you were only with them for a few months. Each child drew a picture of you and stated their appreciations. From Koah "always wears a hat" to "being strong and cute," from "he likes seeing people happy" to "he likes sprint races," from "he speaks another language" to "he likes hugging and watches out for the little ones," the range of admiration prompted you to tuck your chin and hide your shy smile.

During your first week in Canada, you will bite your lip, then slowly walk back and cry, nudged against your mother's hip. You had tried to hug your day teacher goodbye, and uncomfortable, she blocked your approach. School regulations forbade her to touch a child. This is the cold weather of a Canada that is less known abroad, which frostbites the spirit, not merely the tip of your nose.

In a few months, you have learned to write your name, and by osmosis your baby sister can identify the magnetic letters on the fridge door. The *P* of Pai and Paulo. The *M* of Marina, your aunt next door. The *H* of Mamã Heather. On your last Cambra school day, your teacher asked you where you would rather live, "Canada or Portugal?" Her curiosity placed you in the emotionally impossible position of deciding between two loves. A question that you, without hesitation, unwrapped yourself from: "I want to be where my father is going to be."

For dinner preparations on our last afternoon, your grandmother pushes the limits of her Parkinson's-debilitated body and stays on her feet at the stove, for hours stirring the vermicelli and cinnamon in the milk to make the last *aletria*, kneading the potatoes, onion, parsley, and dried cod into oval-shaped deep-fried *bolinhos de bacalhau*, her signature treats, which make her the Nobel laureate in the extended family kitchen lore. We breathe more deeply upon entering the kitchen for our last shared meal with your grandparents, cousins, uncle and aunt, Ti Fernanda and Ti Zé, inhaling the cinnamon-lemony scent of the dessert that contrasts with the pungent fried fish cakes. The fresh eggs from Ti Fernanda's bantams are whisked more thoroughly, and your eyes take in the striking orange of yolks from corn-fed birds. You slow down chewing the wood-baked *padas de Ul*, attempting to impress the bread flavour deeper into the gums, the flesh, the DNA, so as to linger in the mouth, until we sit at our table in Victoria eating bread that does not arrive steaming.

After dinner, we walk across the lane to Ti Fernanda's farm, and you caress the heads of the seven sheep that will not be here the next time you visit. They will be integrated into someone's molecular system after a long Sunday meal and plenty of red wine. These are not your thoughts, for you do not associate land animals with food, having been raised eating the occasional sardine and cod. This meat-free diet is also one of the un-Portuguese traits we share.

The goats will miss you, too, for even now, as your and Amari's excited voices leap over the black tin gate ahead of your steps, the goats, fields away, bleat and congregate at their fence, anticipating the bounty. There are extra collards today for the kid goat, struggling for a chew among the stampede of towering parental legs, as well as for the shy billy rammed by others, never daring to approach the fence for a bite. Your sister, Amari, learning fearlessness from you while the goats tower above her, feeds them the field collards they otherwise can see and smell but never reach.

Now that we have finished packing our suitcases and the red rocking-moose stays rocking to an empty saddle, there will also be aches in reverse. The back and forth of the body requires elasticity of the heart—an essential skill for our future world-village where affections are found continents apart.

We will travel the eight time zones of longing across twenty-four hours of a lit sky, four people crowded into three seats and a tiny aisle, on occasion pacing the aisle and releasing the child energy while trapped in a sky bullet.

The busy first days of integration into Canadian life, unpacking our belongings from storage, will not leave space for sadness to linger. Past patterns will re-emerge, echoes from a life we had placed on pause for five months, as if patterns had hibernated for the winter alongside the bears in the Canadian woods. You will stop your bike on the park trails and crouch when again encountering wild deer prancing through the forest and green spaces of Victoria; you will interrupt plunking pebbles into the water at Clover Point or Willows Beach to admire the elephant seals surfing the skin of the

Pacific, or the otter sewing in the waves with her bobbing motion. The towering cedars and red-skinned arbutus will welcome your hugs as you climb and lie in their arms. Your lungs will recover from the accumulated exhaust of Vale de Cambra and from the factories' spewed metals tainting the valley.

Once again, you will enjoy vegan and vegetarian treats, relishing the array of nut butters in every corner store, the organic this-and-that we eat, even though we will miss the bountiful fruits growing all winter long in your grandparents' garden. You will look forward with added zest this year to running down the deck stairs first thing in the morning to collect red and yellow raspberries for our oatmeal breakfast. The breakfast fruit season will be followed by the cherries, mulberries, currants, elderberries, figs, plums, and apples, growing in our Victoria backyard.

The experience of this sojourn in Portugal will seed a different future in ways we do not yet know. As for your mother and your sister, the trip confined them inside apartment walls for a large slice of the time, as baby Amari sleeps long hours and naps during the afternoon in a season when daylight is short-lived. Nevertheless, there will be echoes to remain in her Portuguese words; she walks around chanting for help, *Ajuda, ajuda.*

You notice me lost in thought after checking over the passports and air tickets for the journey as you sit next to me on the blue couch.

"Why are you listening to such teary music?"

"It's my Portuguese rib."

You pull my shirt up quickly, look on with concern, expecting to encounter an injury. I smile and explain that it is an expression. The Portuguese are said to enjoy the feeling of melancholy.

"But not for too long, okay?"

"I promise," I say, raising my hand solemnly and winking.

I have begun to listen more and more to Mariza's fado, her long wails reverberating in my chest, inoculating the ache yet to come. I putter around the apartment storing toys away, in the end deciding to bring only the clothes I am wearing. I listen to the entire *Fado em Mim* (*The Fado in Me*) album, repeat three times the song "Ó Gente da Minha Terra" ("Oh People of My Land"), until I am fully steeped. Then I reach for the bookshelf and select the Portuguese children's books to bring back to Canada to help keep your second language alive.

In Portugal, in this Caima-watered valley, at the age of four, you experienced your first immersion in TV viewing at your cousins' and grandparents' homes where the screen is left on as a background companion. You became addicted to the instant happiness of chocolate dispensed by your aunt Marina, great-aunt Fernanda, and grandmother Micas. You saw your first movie in a shopping-mall theatre and sat with your cousins for two hours facing a loud giant screen. Sat, yet not in stillness. In the dark, impatient, you soon asked when the film would be over, and once resigned to the long penance, you talked along to the screen action of *Zootopia*.

You saw your first circus with exotic animals drive into town. We visited the grounds.

"Why did they lock the tiger?"

"So he can do tricks for people to enjoy themselves."

"Does the tiger enjoy himself?"

"What do you think?"

You watch the bored tiger sprawled on the wagon floor, not even bothering to lift his head to us when you call.

"Can we open the door?"

"We do not have the keys, Koah."

You did not like seeing the camel and miniature goats behind bars. You wanted to pet them, but I kept you at a distance. The animals stared at us, and we stared back with a blend of curiosity, sadness, and silence. You did not ask to attend the show.

Living these months among extended family scratched alive my wound of separation and longing that had been patched up and dormant for decades. My scar is skin left a little duller for the severed nerves and the break of a smoothly linked pattern across generations.

Next time we return for a few weeks' visit, you will be taller and older, and you may likely connect better to your cousins' sport games. You arrived not knowing what winning was, and now winning matters. You have also learned other languages common to your school mates' culture: elbowing and belittling, shaming and lying, cajoling and laughing at other children's misfortunes.

You will be joyous when you return to this valley again for the unequalled attention you receive in the Portuguese child-loving culture. You are now accustomed to engaging any stranger in conversation, and there is not a day we reach the grocery store on our street without people stopping to talk to you.

The first day in Victoria, you will look at me puzzled after you greet a man passing by and he will not return your greeting.

"Papá, I said hello and the man said nothing."

"It hurts to be ignored. I understand, Koah. Many people in Victoria are not used to being friendly to children. It is sad, isn't it?"

You nod.

A few steps onward, a couple stops to cuddle and baby-talk a terrier walking ahead of us with the same high-pitched tone

Portuguese people use for children. You look at me and shrug when we pass them as if we were invisible. I will read your mind and agree. In Victoria, pets are more important and receive more social attention than children.

Your universe was turned upside down in the duration of a cross-continental flight, a journey that may as well have been diverted to another planet, since these two realities lie galaxies apart. You navigated the turbulent, unknown seas, as an ancient Vasco da Gama of Portuguese historical pride and lore. Except your journey was one of inner discovery and not of conquering, of learning not subjugating, of sharing not profiting. Perhaps you only conquered your fears, learning to leave your comfort zone and stretch your horizon. Yours is a more wholesome journey into the past and the future. The prize is intangible and lifelong. There were moments when I did not know whether I had been sane in having suggested this family adventure overseas. There is a pain that supersedes any pain when I have been the root of another's suffering.

The future will bring us many surprises and unintended consequences arising from your five months' sojourn in the land of your grandparents' birth. If nothing else, I hope you have learned at a visceral level that you carry the resources within to overcome the challenges that will continue to find you.

Over the years, after each visit to Cambra, we also leave behind the seeds for alternative ways of inhabiting the planet. Your great-aunt Fernanda attempted to make *leite creme* using soy milk instead of cow's milk to accommodate your mamma's vegan preference, and she was pleased and surprised by the result. Your grandmother Micas also made *aletria* with soy milk, and all were surprised that cakes could be made without eggs, nodding their enjoyment as they nibbled their first slice baked by your mom. Your papá's *favada* (broad bean stew) replaced the pork pieces and blood sausage with smoked soya and even hesitant Grandfather Agosto asked Grandmother Micas when she could cook the real thing with equal flavour. Old recipes and ways of being demonstrated that traditions could adapt to new sensibilities. This Cambra world that was built across centuries did not collapse.

In the early 1990s, fully vegetarian for the first time, I arrived for an extended visit and your great-uncle José Maria was placed on doctor watch. He dropped in weekly, since it was believed I would not survive a three-month stay without meat. This is a traditional culinary farming culture that cannot easily imagine a meal without animal flesh. So, with each visit, we have been leaving behind other possibilities where the winds of change have difficulty finding the narrow and low lintels of the stone houses.

This evening before our flight to Victoria, and for a last time, I help lock up for the night the many doors of your grandparents' house. I lower the tall heavy iron pole of the gate latch where it rests upright against the granite wall, pointing to the three-dimensional clover-leaf finials decorating the entrance pillar. Over time, that resting, that falling into, has carved a deep groove into the granite stone lip. It is the weight of repetitive gestures; no easy storm will move that which is now caught in its stone cradle. In this case, becoming stuck is a safety matter. This iron pole falling on your head would kill you. I shut the door to the wine-making cellar, holding the grape press and the large granite trough, where grapes have not been trodden in decades. It is now filled with rusty and discarded kitchen appliances, maimed dolls, and a professional hair dryer stand for your grandmother's elaborate Saturday hairdos of the '70s. I also shut the cellar door to the clay slots storing hundreds of empty wine bottles aiding spiders to prop up their silk wall installations.

When I hand your grandfather the jamboree of keys, he tells me this is the last time we will see each other. He has said this on our past three annual visits. We both know the end is near. His will to live is low. I tell him, "If you cannot live for yourself, live for your grandchildren, who need to see you for a lot longer. Your father lived past ninety. Koah and Amari have no other grandfather. They need you as much as they need me." His eyes sparkle again.

Now that I am a father, I taste the tears your grandfather has shed every time I returned to Canada. At the airport or at home, he would be the only one crying. Your aunt Marina and your grandmother Micas wrapped their faces in stoicism. Your grandmother held the ache inside like all her grief, beginning with her mother's premature departure. She will become depressed instead. In those early visiting years, my gaze remained forward only, which avoided the moment and the aches I was triggering. Imagining that this present geographical distance may one day also separate me from you, my son, robs my breath.

The alarm clock rings at 2 a.m. for our journey to the airport. Tomás and Simão stayed up in order to say goodbye, and you and your sister do not want to fall back asleep as we tuck you into your Uncle Filipe's Jeep. The night surrounds you. Rain drums on the windshield, and the wipers labour to erase its traces. The wind whistles, yet not as loudly as the whistling of our speeding vehicle cutting through time. At this hour, the highway is deserted. You and Amari giggle and chat, excited about the trip. Only you can interpret her one-syllable grunts and mumbles, squeaks and screeches. Mamma reads you stories in Portuguese, and for the first few weeks back in Canada, you will speak Portuguese to everybody and be surprised that people do not understand you.

The universe is a roving wind that you learn to stretch your wings for. The ensuing uplifting brings our family closer to our freshly dreamed lives. We will grow wiser in our next visit to my childhood valley and will accept that distances have regrown in our absence, as weeds regrow in a garden left without our daily attention. We will be patient upon our return and allow presence to again refill the space between us. The flowers, scents, and colours will find us once more and bring us the connection, the belonging, and the shared moments in this fragmented history. Lives of cousins, grandparents, great-uncles, and great-aunts that you will occasionally witness, alongside stories relayed from a distance across continents; such stories will be our makeshift bridges for the widening gap of time.

"Can we stay a little longer, Papá?" you ask as we approach the bright airport lights.

"We will return to visit every year, Koah."

When we land again next year, you will be seeking the fond memories we left behind; we will attempt to touch that past magical moment after a childhood year that has passed. We will feel the ache of attempting to recreate scenes that cannot be relived, to play the chicken-aviator game you will have outgrown. We are no longer who we were. No one will be. We will ache until we learn that it is not the family script, not the passing wind, which has long gone, that would bring us what we are seeking. We are seeking a feeling for which we will return and must help build year after year, visit after visit, until the end of our memory.

The Jeep stops, and we empty our luggage onto two overflowing trolleys. Uncle Filipe assists us in manoeuvring the overflowing suitcases to the check-in area while avoiding the darting bodies of latecomers. We join the long lineup and say farewell with a wave of our hands. This time your uncle comes closer and gives you and Amari a long hug that you let yourself sink into.

When Uncle Filipe walks away, your gaze follows him disappearing through the revolving door and back to the Jeep. Your gaze remains suspended in time, even after his outline disappears and there is only an empty revolving door.

acknowledgements

I thank my first readers: Heather S., Avi S., Kate H., Nowick G., Nancy I., Matt J., José R-F., Robin V., Ali B., Judith P., Richard H., Richard T., and Raj S. P. for their generosity with their first impressions.

For financial assistance at the different stages of research, writing, revising, and editing of this manuscript, I am grateful to Calgary Arts Development, the Alberta Foundation for the Arts, and the Canada Council for the Arts.

I would also like to thank the Canadian and international editors and the magazines in which some of these essays previously appeared: *Prairie Fire*, *The Fiddlehead*, *Queen's Quarterly*, *Transitions*, *Reckoning* (USA), *Gávea-Brown* (USA), *Riddle Fence*, and *the other side of hope* (UK).

The essays, "Learning to Shave, Learning to Leave," as well as "Enclosures," received the 2023 and 2020 James H. Gray Award for Short Nonfiction awarded annually by the Writers Guild of Alberta to recognize excellence in essay writing. I thank the Guild and the juries for having been moved by those essays.

I live and write on the lands of the Treaty 7 Peoples: the Blackfoot from Siksika, Kainai, and Piikani; the Dene-Sarcee from Tsuut'ina; and the Stoney-Nakoda from Morley, the Bearspaw, Chiniki, and Wesley First Nations. I also walk in the footsteps of the Métis People from Region 3, Métis Nation of Alberta.

Born in Angola and raised in Portugal, paulo da costa is a bilingual writer, editor, and translator living in the Rocky Mountains of Canada. He is the recipient of the 2020 and 2023 James H. Gray Awards for Short Nonfiction, the 2003 Commonwealth First Book Prize for the Canada-Caribbean Region, the City of Calgary W.O. Mitchell Book Prize, and the Canongate Prize for short fiction. See *paulodacosta.ca*.